LUCKY U, LUCKY US

Utica in the 1950s

By Rodger Potocki

Illustrations by Robert Cimbalo

outskirts
press

For Brian, Phil, and the Owl.

You are still and forever missed.

Table of Contents

Preface

A trip back in time reawakens memories, of good and bad, fun and sorrow, glory and loss, love and rejection, and the values of an era passed. For those of us who lived in it, the remembrance is special, one to forever be valued and appreciated. For the younger, understanding the 1950's may provide a learning experience to guide both the present and future.

The decade was one of contradiction, both nationally and locally. Most who lived and grew up in Utica, New York, consider ourselves lucky to have shared a unique time and place. *Lucky U, Lucky Us,* tells the reader why.

The 1950s are remembered by most as slow-moving, conservative, and rigid. It was all of that, but also a decade of peace, prosperity, and stability. Looking back, many refer to it as "the golden decade." Its blemish, to put it mildly, was racial discrimination and segregation, enforced in the South by law and practiced in the North by conduct and habit.

The decade saw the seeds of major social and political upheaval planted. The Pill, the dream of space travel, a national wiring to television, the legal destruction of segregation, and an entertainment revolution were well underway by its end.

Utica was equally a contradiction. The city was one of well paying, growing jobs, safe neighborhoods and a good deal of flavor and fun. It was also a city under the thumb of political bossism and the influence of organized crime. It too, would experience major change as the 1960's dawned.

This book tells the story of the decade through recorded history interspersed with the author's experiences with the events, characteristics and values of a unique and special time and place.

There are many to thank. The encouragement of friends from the period and the help I received made the book possible. The quality of the contribution from the multi-talented artist Bob Cimbalo in the form of the illustrations he created is priceless. Bob also won the title lottery. Lucky Bob. Dr. David Frisk, a resident scholar at the Alexander Hamilton Institute in nearby Clinton, provided invaluable editing talent.

Sheila Denn Beaton was helpful in providing information, reminding me of memories, while urging the effort to capture them on paper. Sadly, Sheila passed away unexpectedly as the book was being written. My hope is that it's on her reading list in heaven, where she certainly resides.

Most important to the book and author is my wife, Chris, who never wavered in aid, encouragement, and giving when necessary a good kick in the pants.

Rodger Potocki

Prologue

Three men sat in a dark office late one night. A light was on in one room. One of them was an organized crime figure, the second was his lawyer, my uncle Walt, and the third was my father, Walt's younger brother. The idea floated by the crime boss was to knock off a Brinks truck with the help of information provided by an inside man. The insider was to be my father. My father refused, citing his family – a wife and two young kids. He told that tale much later in life.

I have no idea if it was truth or fiction. After all, fiction grows in later years. But it is beyond dispute that Utica's criminal element was real and sown deeply into the city's fabric. It was to play a major role in Utica's political and economic history, which in the decade to come would shake the city down to its very roots. My own roots were part of a simpler fabric.

In the 1940s, my family lived in an apartment in my mother's parents' home in the small Polish section of East Utica. Another sibling an uncle of ours, and his family lived in a similar apartment on that same floor. Bathrooms were shared with cousins, and baths were taken once a week in a steel tub of water heated on the kitchen stove. Our grandmother watched we kids while our parents worked. My grandfather walked to work at a knitting mill on Broad Street. It took one of his fingers. He missed two days of work.

One neighbor was a quiet, nice guy who often traveled out of town. In very hushed terms, many suggested he was a mob hit man who did all of his work out of town. It may have all been imagined, as so much neighborhood gossip is, but everyone sure felt safe.

My recollections of that time and place are limited, but some stand out. I clearly recall my uncles Milt and Louie entering the house wearing their service uniforms. Louie was at Pearl Harbor on a ship that was bombed. Milt was an Army captain. At Milt's funeral, when he died at 100, one of his sons read a letter signed by every soldier under his father's command shortly after the war. In very moving terms, they said they would follow him anywhere, anytime. He must have been one hell of a leader. That, most would never guess. His quiet demeanor and warm smile left one hard-put to imagine him in combat. Many of the Greatest Generation did not wear their bravery on their sleeves or talk much about their days fighting for their country. They did not trumpet their bravery or sacrifice. But when I witnessed their return, not really knowing them or even what they did, I was in awe.

We kids had three weekly treats to enjoy: gathering around the radio to listen to "The Shadow," taking an empty pot to get it filled at Spaghetti Joe's on Pellettieri Avenue and Jay, and Sunday car rides to see how the rich people lived on the Memorial Parkway and in South Utica.

I recall our "poorer" neighborhood as a lot of fun, not run-down, not at all as one begging for escape. My mother, who grew up at the 1007 same Jay St. house had aspirations to move to what she considered "up in the world." Many of her age, stage of life, and family history had the same aspiration. After all, America was the land of opportunity.

In our neighborhood, the polka music blared from the nearby Polonia Hall most nights, and families spent a good deal of time sitting on the porch stoops. In the summertime, when it got really hot, the firemen opened the hydrants for us to run under the shooting, cold water. We little ones ran through the water screaming and screeching, while groups of parents and grandparents sat around talking and keeping a close eye on us.

The vegetable cart man came by, shouting his wares in sing-song verse. The ice man appeared weekly to refill the ice that cooled the icebox. Ours was Frank Dulan, who my father knew well from school and ball-playing days. He was a jovial sort and full of the blarney.

This slice of Jay was a neighborhood of fun, play, and close relationships. We kids even joked with the neighborhood drunk who regularly staggered out of the Polonia. My memories are of laughter, a sense of the comfort, and the enjoyment of living in a close community. All houses were well-kept, with gardens in small backyards. My grandfather tended a cherry tree, and I once saw my grandmother cut off the head of a chicken as her first step in cooking it. But life on Jay was not a full bowl of cherries.

School was at St. Stanislaus, a Polish Catholic school on Nickel Street not far from Bleecker, within walking distance from our house. My mother had attended there and was a favorite of the nuns. She and her mother in earlier days helped the nuns clean the church every weekend, but that closeness did not soothe the image of rigid, fierce nuns lodged in my mind. My sister recalls their softer side and often claims to have been a favorite. I was not. I was far too afraid of their wrath.

The nuns spoke in Polish and broken English. Assimilation certainly was not their goal. If a student was caught swearing, he was forced to eat soap. If you were left- handed, you were of the Devil and forced to write right-handed. The girls were viewed much more as saints than the boys.

Every so often a Utica policeman would show up, to mete out punishment for misbehavior as documented by the principal. Those punished were ridiculed in front of all. I was so petrified of the sisters and of the system that I rarely spoke. I was taken for a well-behaved, shy boy, but was actually just scared to death by the whole scene. I was not alone – most were also attending school in fear. But classrooms were sure silent, except for the instruction.

Imagine how I felt when I learned that I was to be one of the few kids, perhaps the only one, in the annals of St. Stan's to flunk kindergarten. A petty neighborhood mother made a complaint that I was too young to advance to the first grade. Technically she was correct. So the school that allowed me to start too young in the first place then disallowed me from advancing. My mother was furious at the neighbor and at the school. She was never, throughout her 97 years, to forgive either. My grandmother, who loved the church and school, never said a word.

That grandmother, Felicia, was outwardly tough and could deliver a hard broom swat to the posterior. Underneath it all, she was loving too, and proud of her family, especially us young ones.

Grandfather Ignaz worked extremely hard, never learned English, and was a man of few words. His joy was his daily shot of whiskey, with a beer chaser, and his grandkids. He smiled as he drank and was a warm, and nice guy who was still dazzled by America. I eventually learned that this good man married my grandmother knowing she was pregnant by another. I was told that much later in life, after the deaths of both grandparents. My mother held a special, deep love for her father and wished to be buried next to him. I was not surprised, knowing and understanding his strength. He did not have to say much for his goodness to be understood. I loved him a good deal, and regret never telling him so. An older me did frequently pat him on the head and squeeze his shoulders. I hope that was enough.

My grandmother spoke broken English and urged us daily to become American. Not speaking Polish was part of the drill. The goal of immigrants in those years was to assimilate as quickly and completely as possible. Immigrant grandparents longed to have their grandkids become not only Americans but successful, professional Americans. To my grandmother, that meant a good education and discarding Polish ways. The idea that one or more of us could become a teacher, lawyer, or doctor was her dream. My parents, particularly my mother, bought into that dream, pushed it hard on us, and preached the importance of aspiration with both enticement and force.

The new decade would start for my family in a new house in a new neighborhood, one that was purely "American." It was time to leave the old and begin the new. We were all ready and excited to leave the cocoon of the grandparents' house in the Polish sliver of East Utica. It was time to "move up." It was time to discard ethnic roots and to grab hold of the American dream.

CHAPTER 1

The Nation

The National Setting

Utica in the 1950s can be fully understood only as part of the larger national picture. If America at the time could be summarized with one phrase, a most accurate one, it would be: the decade of Ike.

General, then President Eisenhower was the 1950s. He was "square." In the vernacular of a bit later in the decade, being square meant being quiet, steady, traditional, and driven to get ahead – with a little boring thrown in. Ike was all of that.

He ended the Korean War, was not bombastic like President Truman, and was not a narcissist of the Douglas MacArthur type. MacArthur was another military hero of the period who took on Truman and paid the price; he got fired.

The general did get huge parades but wound up as he predicted, an old soldier who faded away.

Ike was elected president in 1952 over the politically hapless Adlai Stevenson, who gained the Democratic nomination when Truman lost New Hampshire and bowed out. The war hero candidate promised to "go to Korea" to end that conflict. His key role in winning World War ll gave his pledge a level of credibility no one seriously questioned. As the ditty went, to the tune of "Whistle While You Work": "Eisenhower's got the power, Stevenson's a jerk." Kid at our school sang it.

Ike ended the war in 1953, by negotiating a split of Korea that exists to this day. The solution was similar to the split of Vietnam after the French were driven out. History has proven those decisions to be questionable. Both wars resulted in over 50,000 Americans being killed, and the troop commitment in Korea continues even today. Sixty-four years later, our troops still sit in the middle of a powder keg. At this book's writing, the possibility of peace has developed but the threat of a future Korean conflict still exists. Another aspect of Korea is that it may have been the first war America fought without the goal of complete victory.

The country after World War II was sick of war. Korea was our first war that was not declared by Congress; it was fought as a police action of the relatively young United Nations. If we were forced to declare war, it is likely that public opinion would have been against it. It became clear by the end of the 1950s that various types of undeclared war would become acceptable to Americans and their government.

By 1949, we entered yet another kind of war, the Cold War, when the Russians tested their atomic bomb and reneged on their promise of free elections in Eastern Europe. The clash with communism was born. As our newspapers put it well into the '50s, the "Reds" were the enemies of our country and our way of life. Khrushchev gave his "We will bury you" speech in Moscow in 1956. With atomic weapons in the Russian arsenal, the threat was not to be taken lightly in the United States.

The world was upside down, without Americans realizing it at the time. The Western democracies fought a world war ignited by the invasion of Poland by the Nazis, only to see that country then controlled by the Russians, along with most of the rest of Eastern Europe.

We appeared to trade one totalitarian enemy for another at immense cost. Our new enemy was Russia, our ally during the hot war. The Red scare was real in the sense that two very different political/economic systems, capitalism and communism, vied to become the model for the rest of the world. The stakes were high, with unprecedented danger due to the possibility of atomic mass destruction. Air raid alerts, with kids diving under desks in elementary school, became routine. Hitler and the Nazi nightmare were gone, but the hammer and sickle posed an enormous threat to the free world. America did not blink at the task ahead. We moved into high economic gear.

With a war hero president who was the picture of calm stability, and a capitalistic economic system producing cheap energy and new products envied around the world, Americans were proud, excited, and confident about the future. We did not seriously question our dominance as the supreme world power. As winners of two world wars, we were certainly ready to win the peace. After all, we were the good guys. But not all of our leaders were accepted as such.

One of the more famous examples of domestic Cold War clashes was the Joe McCarthy-Eisenhower brawl, which came to a head in 1954. An early part of the televised political theater so common and familiar to us now was the hearings held by Senator McCarthy's committee when it looked into communist activities in the Army. McCarthy crossed the line when he claimed that even Ike was sympathetic to communism. He was asked during a public hearing: "Sir, have you no shame?" That deflated and quickly ended his career. McCarthy died a broken man. Decades later, Russian documents revealed that he was more right than wrong about communist sympathizers imbedded in our government and those of other democracies.

It borders on the bizarre that as this book is being written, Russian influence within the American government has resurfaced. History does indeed tend to repeat itself.

The Economy

As the boys came home, first from Europe and then the Pacific and finally from Korea, they went back to work at the jobs they had left, also filling the many new ones being created. By the early '50s, stores selling the new rage, television sets, were expanding by a staggering 1,000 per month nationwide. Everyone who watched at a friend's or neighbors, or who spied one playing in a store window, wanted one. Production and sales soared, as did the number of companies making TVs. What did this mean? Jobs and entertainment. The television boom was just one of the new products and building construction techniques spurring major economic expansion. A shift from a cash-driven to a credit-driven society was also transformational as an economic stimulant. The first credit card was introduced in 1950, and by the end of the decade consumers became used to using them. Consumer spending and debt soared relative to the past.

The GI Bill spurred home buying and education, while Ike's federal highway spending contributed to increased prosperity marked by an economic growth of 37 percent GDP growth in the decade. This, along with Eisenhower's frugality, led to a balanced federal budget, something that was to become a relic of the past soon after the decade ended.

A significant feature of the national economy was that defense spending was not drastically cut, as in other postwar periods. The Cold War and anti-communism demanded continued military spending. We kept producing more advanced weapons, maintained a large military force, and undertook advanced research in weapons development, intelligence tools, and military strategy. Troops were kept in Korea, Western Europe, in Japan. The effort to modernize everything from tanks to planes to bombs was immense. The military-industrial complex Ike was to take note of as he was leaving office at the decade's end was thriving even at its start.

New styles and technologies were driving automobile production, clothing, and communications networks. Computers were born. But the most important economic feature of all was the housing boom. Men no longer at war, and women back home from the factories they worked at when the men were gone, were having babies and plenty of them. The little darlings came to be known as baby boomers.

This growth of the family led to an explosion of housing demand. Demand, in turn, drove new methods of construction. The housing market and all of its many offshoots grew quickly and mightily. Entire new communities like Levittown were born. The urge to migrate from crowded cities to more spacious suburban settings itched the psyches of parents seeking more open space.

Religion

Today, as the practice of religion and even the belief in a God seriously decline, it is difficult to imagine that a priest was a major TV star in the '50s. Bishop Fulton J. Sheen's "Life Is Worth Living" was watched by millions. Most Americans were regular attendees at churches and synagogues. Sixty- eight percent of Americans went to a religious service at least once a week. This basic religious devotion was also evidenced in conduct, entertainment, and styles of dress. Manners, modesty, clean living, and clean language were prevalent, particularly in the first half of the decade. They were largely driven by religious convictions and practices. Religion, belief in God, and religious community organizations and services to others were staples of American society. Government was small and limited, not yet stepping in to replace local charities in "helping thy neighbor." But the pious were not without sin.

Societies anytime, anywhere, under any system are never totally pure. Virtually everyone drank alcohol, many to the extreme. And there were "discreet" affairs of the body and the heart, not halted by attending religious services. The '50s were not immune to hypocrisy.

"Peyton Place", a novel released in 1956, was a national hit that was believed, by many, to present a true picture of the social behavior of the time. A divorce rate of under 29 percent suggests that claim was questionable.

The "Peyton Place" America was largely an exaggerated fiction. Moral standards, by and large, were rigid. Those who lived through the '50s are staggered by the differences today. Porn, for example, hidden under the counter then, is now a very public multi-billion dollar industry. What was unthinkable then is now the norm. In 1955, anyone running around disputing what constitutes gender, the definition of marriage, or separate locker rooms for men and women would most likely have been labeled as mentally ill and condemned in every corner of society.

Entertainment

What could be cleaner, more innocent, and more decent than the Nelson family as depicted on the hit TV show "Ozzie and Harriet"? That was family life portrayed on TV. Perry Como, Uncle Milty, "I Love Lucy," Gary Cooper in "High Noon" ruled the day. There was crystal- clear definition of the good guys and bad guys. Moral clarity dominated on the surface of daily life. Censorship regulated both the movie and TV industries. But beneath the surface, the rumblings of change grew louder as the decade wore on.

The Cold War and communism pushed the country toward not only the hot war of Korea but domestic anti-communist fervor as well. Hollywood blacklisting of people thought to be communist sympathizers took hold. For example, the screen writer of "High Noon" was to be blacklisted, left the U.S., and wrote future screenplays under a fake name. The wonderful and everlasting "The Bridge On the River Kwai" was one of his achievements under that name. Censorship took on several forms and affected all entertainment venues, including the printed word.

Comedy on the relatively new medium of television was both brilliant and clean. Martin and Lewis was the hottest act in America in the early '50s, and their TV show was a smash hit. "Your Show of Shows" featuring Sid Caesar, Imogene Coca, Carl Reiner, and others, which ran in the first half of the decade, was among the best and most creative comedy of all time. Not a swear word was spoken, not a sex joke made. A shift started in the second half of the decade.

Rock and Roll really began early, not later, in the decade[Is this OK?] with the blend of rhythm and blues largely found in black music plus white country music with new guitar and sax sounds added, a blend that created a new genre of dance and of message. The message was largely about love, rejection, and loss.

Later in the '50s, the beatniks and rebels of the James Dean and Marlon Brando antihero types were popularized. Elvis burst onto the scene in 1956. Chuck Berry put the sensuous guitar and more risqué lyrics into rock, as the strict diet of love ballads ended. As Bob Dylan was to write in the next decade, the times were changing. The changes which were to explode during the '60s took root in the 1950s. In this sense, the decade of clarity and "the square" was laying the groundwork for the decade of rebellion and confusion.

Authors

Hemingway was the rage. Among the other best and most popular authors were Steinbeck, O'Hara, Uris, James Jones, Drury, Michener, and Boris Pasternak. Others of more limited and cultish fame, such as Ayn Rand and J.D. Salinger, wrote books, including "Atlas Shrugged," that were later to bloom in popularity and would have an impact on people for generations to come. Salinger's first book, "Catcher in the Rye" published in 1951, sells about a million copies a year today. Pasternak internationalized American popular book tastes with the unforgettable "Doctor Zhivago." Readers may also remember the explosion during the '50s of books turning into movies. Steinbeck's

"East of Eden" and Rose's "Twelve Angry Men" may be the most famous, although perhaps not the very best. My vote would go to "The
Old Man and the Sea," the Hemingway novel presented to the movie
audience with the great Spencer Tracy in the lead.

Film

Music, movies, actors and actresses will be discussed in more detail
later in the book. But one especially critical feature in films, and thus
in the entertainment of the time, was the introduction of color. The
'50s brought the end of black and white, as the 1920s ended the era of
silent movies with "talkies." Some of American film history's greatest
directors, screenwriters, and actors and actresses graced the decade's
theaters (mixed with many so many bad movies that would later be
viewed as "camp"). The previously mentioned "High Noon" of 1952,
and James Dean's "Rebel Without a Cause" several years later, would
become classics. "High Noon," one of the last great black and white
films, was also black and white in the sense that it clearly depicted
its hero Will Kane, played by Cooper, as a man of duty, courage, and
justice. The Dean movie, and others such as "On the Waterfront" and
"The Men" starring Marlon Brando, were not as black and white. The
nudge toward the antihero had arrived.

Sex and Behavior

Sex was not casual, and the relationship between sexual behavior
and religion was significantly stronger than it is today. Birth control
devices were not sold in drugstore display cases; you had to ask.
"The pill," although formulated, was not yet in use. Abortion was
illegal. If your high school sweetheart got pregnant, you usually married. There were statistically few single-parent homes. The divorce
rate was low at under 20%, and rarer among the middle class and the
poor. Divorce was more a tool of the rich and famous, and even they
treaded lightly. With a culture where men did not swear in front of
women and dress was modest, there was no full nudity, even in the
newly hatched Playboy. If a woman was not married by 20, she had

the fear of being labeled an old maid. Most women had returned to the role of homemaker after the big war, while men dominated the workplace.

There were women pioneers in many fields, including politics, but they were rare. Being a mother, homemaker, church volunteer, and preparer of the family dinner was the feminine norm.

Race

While it has often been said that the '50s was a great decade, a "golden" one in our history, the phrase "if you were white" could be added. In the South, blacks were still being lynched and for little reason other than skin color. Segregation was the Southern way of life. Ike sent troops into Little Rock to enforce the Supreme Court- ordered integration of schools, but the South resisted at every turn. The Northern segregation model was different, but evil and unfair as well.

Living space and other locations were segregated by zoning, economics, and attitudes. Officially integrated Northern schools were segregated by intentional policies that directed black students to shop, trades, and secretarial classes while discouraging them from college preparatory classes. Neighborhoods were largely all- black or all-white.

The striking aspect of the race question in the North was how little we knew what was going on in the South, and how little we thought about what we were doing in our own part of the country. The Northern indifference toward blacks was more subtle, but in many ways even more offensive, than forcing people to sit in the back of the bus.

That discriminatory tradition in the South came under fire in 1955, with the start of the Montgomery Bus Boycott which erupted in response to the treatment of Rosa Parks. A hardline Southern segregationist at the time, Birmingham police commissioner Bull Connor, would become the face of racism by the early '60s. The use of dogs and firehoses on civil rights protesters there in the mid-sixties would become the TV image of the South that awakened the nation.

The Underworld Surfaces

Drugs, opiates, random street shootings, and outbreaks of home invasions were virtually unheard of in Utica and most other communities. Crime centered on gambling, prostitution, loan sharking, union manipulations and theft, political bribery, bid-fixing, and insider land deals. Americans learned in the late '40s and early '50s that organized crime was indeed part of the national landscape. The nation was riveted to the Kefauver hearings in Washington, which exposed the existence of La Cosa Nostra, the Mafia, for the first time. But many people, including J. Edgar Hoover's FBI, did not acknowledge a nationally organized Mafia. Later in the decade, an event was to take place that would shock both Utica and the country.

In 1957, Italian-American crime figures from across the land gathered in the little village of Apalachin in southern New York State. A trooper stumbled onto it. That meeting verified what the earlier Kefauver congressional hearings had uncovered about an extensive nationwide syndicate. Most of the nation's top Mafia figures had traveled there to sort out conflicts of crime families and territory.

Three present at the "Apalachin Convention" were from Utica: Joe Falcone, Salvatore Falcone, and Rosario Mancuso. These revelations, which would eventually result in major change and transition for the city, will be discussed at greater length later in the book. I had previously met Joe Falcone, in a somewhat amusing way.

By the mid-'50s, I was a Utica Daily Press newspaper delivery boy. One cold morning I delivered to one of my regular spots, Saint Elizabeth Hospital, and noticed nurses gathered at a station on one floor, all abuzz. I stopped to check in, which was my normal procedure before I went room-to-room to hawk the paper. I also loved to stop and flirt with the cute nurses. That morning I got a shock and an immediate greedy thought.

Joseph Falcone had been admitted the night before. My eyes lit up as my hopes soared. Of course this famous mob guy, who probably lights his cigars with $20 bills, would tip me as I was never tipped before. I could envision it all: "Here, kid, take this ten-spot and see me tomorrow." I asked his room number. When I got there, I gently knocked and heard a graveled voice say, "Come on in." Here he was slightly sitting up in bed, a silver-haired, somewhat little-looking guy who also looked pretty sick. I asked him if he wanted a paper. Yes. The paper was 7 cents a copy and he handed me a dime. His hand stayed out for the 3 cents change! The bubble of the freewheeling, big-spending mobster had burst. As a kid, I did not fully understand the connection he had, or could have had, with local politics and how that affected my city. The paper I was delivering had already begun to seriously cover, and rail against, government corruption and vice in the city. But no formal relationships involving organized crime had been seriously investigated or exposed.

Politics

The nation was more Republican, but Utica was Democrat. Not only was the city Democrat; it was also controlled by a longtime political boss, Rufus Elefante. "Rufie" rose to power in the late '20s allied with the local Irish and Jewish politicians and businessmen, expanded his power and influence in the '30s – which included a close relationship with President Roosevelt – and pretty much had unlimited political power in the late '40s and throughout the '50s. His value in politics was based on turning out the largest voting bloc in the area, the Utica Italian vote. The Depression was key to his rise, since patronage jobs were like gold and could be converted into both more votes and sources of political contributions.

By the late 40's and early '50s, some speculated that Elefante had forged a relationship with organized crime in Utica that resulted in a wide-open city. Police appeared to turn a blind eye (at the very least) to the two major criminal enterprises of the time in Utica, gambling and prostitution. A relationship between Elefante and the mob was never proven. Financial connections were never substantiated. In fact, Rufie was never charged with a crime, although later in the decade close associates were. But part of the ambiance of the city, which was both alluring in some ways and destructive in others, was one of frequent flirtation with vice and crime.

Utica was perceived as a Cherokee Strip type of city where mobsters from other places would not be hassled. For example, one major New York City crime figure, Albert Anastasia, was a fairly regular visitor. In one instance, my family was involved in a near-comical way.

My parents were close friends with a police captain and his wife. Both parents often told the story of the night they went to Vernon Downs, a recently opened racetrack outside of the city, with their friends and a guest, Mr. Anastasia, the major New York crime figure. The story went that Anastasia could not win a race. At one point he ripped up some losing tickets, threw them, and shouted: "This is harder than robbin' a fuckin' bank!"

The point is that the line between the cops and the robbers was thin. The question always asked but never answered is the extent of the marriage between politics and organized crime figures.

This national-local link played a key part in both the city's success and its eventual decline as the decade ended.

It should be understood that Democratic boss politics and its close relationships with crime were not unique to Utica. New York City, Albany, Buffalo, places like Kansas City, St. Louis, New Orleans, Las Vegas, and others had similar characteristics under which politics and organized crime at least dated if not married. And most of these cities boomed during the period. Life in the fast lane was usually marked by economic prosperity along with flawed morality. Political control by the few along with criminal enterprise provided thrills, money, recreation so to speak, and a certain decadence. It was a mixed bag for many urban areas, including Utica. To this day, many who recall it view the period of political boss control and Mafia presence as a positive one in the city's history. It will be discussed more later in the book.

Lifestyle

Men who did not work with their hands wore ties and jackets to their jobs, to church, and to dinner at home. Everyone got dressed up in their Sunday best for church. Nearly all attended church or temple at least once a week. Women did not swear, just as men didn't in front of women. TV was black and white, with only two or three channels. There were but a few suburban shopping malls, in their infancy. Downtowns were the centers of commercial and social life. Families that owned a car had just one. It was not that unusual not to own one. A large number of immigrants never learned how to drive. Two-family homes, "flats", were common, as was renting. A one-family home with an acre of land in the suburbs was still an unrealized part of the American dream for most. Hard work was valued – and necessary in order to get ahead. The government safety net was small, mainly limited to Social Security for the elderly. Receiving "relief," as welfare was called, was viewed as shameful. Most people started work at age 14, with part-time and summer jobs. Many mothers were stay-at-home moms. The majority of both sexes did not go to college. Those women who did went to teachers' colleges or nursing schools. Music was not a big part of life. Most homes' doors were not locked at night. Kids played in the street. Manners and respect for one's elders were etched into people at an early age. It was always "Mr." and "Mrs." until you were told otherwise. These were a few and important characteristics of life in the '50s.

In most ways, life in Utica mirrored life in the rest of America. In some ways it did not. In certain telling ways it was unique, more interesting and more complicated.

14

CHAPTER 2

Utica

The City - Industry and Business

The heart of a community is its economy. A vibrant economic base creates interest, appeal, creativity, opportunity and enjoyment. It offers the dignity of work, of providing for oneself and one's family. Hard work was one of the pillars of the Utica community from its foundation to the decade of the '50s.

The soul of a community is its culture.

Culturally, Utica was a healthy, religious, colorful tapestry of European ethnic variety founded by the Anglo-Saxons and Irish and later expanded by the waves of Italian, Polish and German immigration.

The city's historical blend of Anglo-Saxon entrepreneurial talent and the risk-taking and the work-to-the-bone craftsmanship and drive of its German, Italian and Polish immigrants melded into a robust center of commerce. Geographic factors and political decision making, including the location of rivers, the Erie Canal, railways and eventually major roadways, played large roles in this economic success story.

By 1950, Utica had made the transition from the knitting capital of the world to an economy anchored by defense-oriented companies.

World War II and the Cold War were, from an economic viewpoint, kind to Utica. Jobs and money generated by the wartime economy continued to flow throughout the decade of the 50's. Many of these companies were also creating spinoff, consumer-directed products.

Our major industry was General Electric, which through that period employed a workforce of 10,000. Most were city residents. The company's main facility was on French Road, while it also occupied large spaces in old knitting mill buildings on Broad Street. A stone's throw from the main GE plant stood Bendix Aviation, on a large site bordered by French Road and Seward Avenue.

On the east side of the city were Chicago Pneumatic, Savage Arms, and Drop Forge, and in Ilion there was Remington Arms. All were healthy and thriving companies.

A most important employer for Utica and the entire area was the growing Griffiss Air Force Base, located in Rome. The base was established in 1942 and had been expanding ever since.

It was delivered to the area in no small part by the political relationship between Utica's Democratic Party leader, Rufus Elefante, and President Roosevelt. Elefante had delivered significant votes to FDR and raised healthy amounts of political donations from the outset of the president's political career. The former New York governor also had a warm feeling for his home state and its ethnic mix. It is a reasonable assumption that the area would never have been awarded the base without the FDR-Elefante connection.

A Utica attorney, William Bray, was lieutenant governor for part of FDR's presidential years and was also in the local Democratic machine. Our political influence on this high level was as strong as, or stronger than, that of most Upstate areas. There is no question that the prime mover of this influence and political strength was Elefante. And I would later benefit from Mr. Bray's kind gesture on my behalf.

In 1961, he wrote a letter of recommendation for me for admission to his alma mater, Colgate University. Mr. Bray carried weight. His recommendation was the result of a favor urged by Mrs. Bray, who had her hair done at the Boston Store beauty salon, which was managed by my mother. This connection between hair styling and a successful entry to a choice school with the help of political influence offers a valuable lesson: Ask and ye may receive. Or in better terms, never be afraid to network.

In the 1950s both the Air Force base and Elefante saw their zenith in influence and power, one economic and the other political. Griffiss employed over 7,000 people and Elefante had total control of Utica's, if not the entire political and governmental apparatus of the area.

The city's economy was diversified by a number of healthy home-grown companies not dependent on the defense industry.

Some of these included Bosserts, Utica Cutlery, and Utica Club, now the Matt's Brewing Company, all mainstays of West Utica. There was also a foundation of local banks, including the Savings Bank of Utica, the Oneida National Bank, and the Bank of Utica, that were wealthy and influential, locally and statewide. Home-grown investment money and decisions about how to use it were instrumental to growth in commerce and jobs.

Clearly the bulk of the management talent so important to the city, in terms of both direct and indirect effect on community life, was coming from the large defense companies and these home-grown companies. Interestingly, though, this talent was not frequently lent to city government and politics.

Utica was also a significant legal center. Its law firms served clients locally, statewide and nationally. One, for example, the Kernan and Kernan firm, represented the New York State Central Rail Company.

The city's retail and commercial character is more fully described in the next section. For now, let it suffice to say that Utica was the commercial center and hub of the region. People from a relatively large radius shopped, dined and were entertained in our downtown.

A healthy share of the Utica economy was what would now be called the "underground economy." Prostitution, gambling and theft meant off-the-books money and jobs that flowed freely. In this sense, crime paid. Vice protected if not encouraged by politicians, for the obvious reasons of money and power, was a Utica staple. The city's vice industry was a topic civic leaders, most businessmen, the clergy and the ordinary citizen avoided. It was the Utica newspapers that first brought the issue into the public arena beginning in the late '40s. This anti-corruption crusade, waged over a long period and combined with national events such as the Apalachin Convention, profoundly affected the community. The Utica papers were skilled and relentless in exposing corruption and pushing for political reform. That would all come to a head by the end of the 1950s.

Utica was a densely populated city featuring neighborhoods that reflected its ethnic makeup, industry and economy. The movement to the suburbs was in its infancy and had not yet negatively impacted the center city. For city dwellers, the suburbs were cow country. Even nearby Rome was considered an inferior, backwater town.

City Neighborhoods

It is easiest to understand Utica in the '50s by describing its neighborhoods and their ethnic makeup. For this section, the "American" suffix is dropped in describing the various ethnic groups. For example, an Italian-American is described as an Italian.

A main characteristic of 1950s Utica was its near-total whiteness. Of a population of about 112,000, only 1.6 percent were black. There were no other nonwhite minority groups. Blacks were for all practical

purposes segregated in most aspects of city life. The breakup of eth-
nic-dominated and ethnically separated neighborhoods, already taking place in other American and New York state cities, was slower in
coming to Utica.

East Utica was overwhelmingly Italian. West Utica was predominantly
Polish, and South Utica, Irish. A section more or less in the center of
the city north of the Parkway was a mixed white neighborhood called
Cornhill. Most of the city's Jewish residents were in South Utica.

A majority of the black population lived in public housing, north of
the downtown, separated from it by Oriskany and Broad streets. The
Washington Courts public housing project was entirely black.

Downtown, as it is now, was in the middle of the city. It was more
linear than compact, stretching the full length of Genesee Street from
Oriskany Street to the Stanley Theater, over a half a mile.

There was a North Utica, but it was more of a newer area with few
people. City infrastructure extensions such as public water service
were underway, but not yet to an extent that was drawing a significant
population there.

Each section of the city had its own neighborhood elementary schools,
both public and Catholic, distinctive ethnic restaurants, and other
businesses, along with strong remnants of the European cultures from
which their populations sprang. Personal interactions between residents of different neighborhoods were limited.

Two public high schools were available in the city: Utica Free
Academy and Proctor High School. Two Catholic high schools, Saint
Francis and Utica Catholic Academy, served that religious community.
The Catholic schools were tiny relative to the public UFA, which had
a student body of about 2,500 compared with the Catholic schools'
fewer than 1,000. Proctor, however, was also on the small side. The

high schools, except Proctor, were in central locations fairly close to the downtown. There were no school buses. Students walked, took city buses or were driven by parents. Only a handful of students had cars.

UFA was as diverse as could be, since its students represented all of Utica. Proctor was predominantly Italian, with a small group of kids from my old former little Polish area in East Utica. The Catholic schools educated students who sought a religious education. All students were white. Blacks went to UFA, my high school. I knew of none at Proctor when I was a student, in the last half of the '50s. There were two black Proctor students in the early part of the decade, a brother and sister.

Every neighborhood had a certain charm, character and flavor in things from housing type to eating places, churches to language mix. All neighborhoods were safe. Crime was nearly nonexistent. Kids could play in the streets, ride their bikes to playgrounds, and go to a neighborhood store for a soda or ice cream—on their own, from seven or eight years of age on. Popular neighborhood movie houses like the Rialto, Family, Uptown, Oneida and Lincoln were well-attended by people of all ages. These theaters featured special showings such as Saturday morning cartoons and Westerns for kids, and evening "dish giveaway specials" for adults at night. Socially, neighborhoods were self-contained. Most young people and adults did not cross neighborhood lines unless they were visiting relatives.

The heavily Italian east side was the largest and most interesting part of the city. It featured the best and most well-known Italian restaurants, like the original Grimaldi's, Frankie Nash's, Ventura's, Pescatore's, and other less well-known but also great dining places. Poles living in their slice of the east side gathered at Skiba Post, danced at the Polonia Hall, and prayed at St. Stanislaus church. Their children climbed up the stairs to tiny classrooms for their education. The better-known restaurants like Grimaldi's, located close to the downtown, even served the "mayonnaise" Irish people from South Utica. You would never find one at the Polonia.

The Italian festivals at Mt. Carmel and St. Anthony's churches and on Jay Street were rousing, packed with people, great food and music, and full of good will. Hindu sold clams at his stand on Mohawk and Bleecker, while Italian bakeries and coffee shops were gathering places for politicians, mobsters, lawyers and folks just getting together. Bleecker, stretching all the way to the fringe of downtown, was jammed with a variety of Italian-flavored commercial activity. The Florentine and Caruso's were packed with shoppers and interesting characters. Most of these places were dominated by male customers, except for the takeout bakery bread and specialty cookie traffic. If you were lucky, or of the in-crowd, you were treated to laughs and wonderful tales.

From a young age on, I was struck by the fun and good nature of the Utica Italian community. It could be argued that this time, the '50s, was the high point of the Italian influence on the city.

Playgrounds were plentiful, and the public Buckley swimming pool could be accessed by bus or foot. As little kids, my sister and I, along with other youngsters on Jay Street, walked to the pool bringing our mayonnaise sandwiches for lunch or a snack. In later years, my sister was to lifeguard there. It actually wasn't a happy place for me, given my disdain for the cold water. I was so thin that my bones rattled every time I went in. But oh, I loved mayonnaise sandwiches.

Lincoln Avenue was the center of the west side. There stood the majestic Holy Trinity Church, the iconic Bazan's bakery, and the Polish Community Club a few blocks away. Polish stores like Hapanowicz Meat Market and Pulaski Market were close by. Interestingly, there were few if any Polish restaurants. Why? Polish food is time-consuming to prepare. That meant that full Polish dinners consisting of golabki, pierogi, kapusta (cabbage) and nalesniki were served at home, at churches, and at Polish clubs where ladies took time to prepare the food. Often it was served to raise money for churches or groups advancing Polish culture. Pierogis and kielbasa and kapusta sandwiches were served at most bars. As the equivalent of the Sunday Italian family dinner, the Polish homes served plates of ham, cabbage and pierogi.

West End kids gathered at Lincoln Playground and Murnane Field which also hosted adult baseball leagues and was Utica Free Academy's home baseball, track and football field. Addison Miller park featured a public pool for the west side and also offered a baseball field and basketball courts.

The fabric of the Polish community was held together by the Holy Trinity church and the Polish Community Club. Men bonded at neighborhood bars. Cards, shuffleboard, jukeboxes, beer, sandwiches and pickled eggs were offered at relatively small and lively, mostly male hangouts. Two that stick out as the "in" places were the Rainbow Grill on Varick Street and Gilberti's on Columbia Square. Both will be discussed in greater detail later in the book.

The Rainbow bridged generations. My father hung out there when he was younger. From him, I learned that the nickname for the place in those days was "The Bucket of Blood," due to the many fights. The fights stemmed from two main sources. "The Bow" was located right next to the Utica Club Brewery, whose workers would drink there after work. On occasion, work disputes would break out into fights. In addition, there were sometimes harsh disputes between ethnic groups, particularly Poles and Italians.

Cornhill was a middle-class area of families representing a mixture of ethnic types. This neighborhood was different in the sense that it did not feature many ethnic restaurants and was less commercial than other sections. Its housing was not fancy, mostly two-family or small one-family homes, but most was in top-notch condition. In fact, residents of all Utica neighborhoods took great pride in their living space.

Property maintenance meant a lot to most residents of Utica who were still connected to the European immigration wave. Having a house or a flat in America was something of which to be proud. Neighborhood pride was fierce, shared and enforced. Anyone falling short of acceptable standards of property upkeep heard about it from their neighbors. A legion of code inspectors was not needed. Neighborhood pride ruled.

South Utica, which would be my home for most of the decade, was split in two from a socioeconomic standpoint. Genesee was the divide. The side extending east of the street was upscale; the side running west of it was middle-class. The housing on the upscale side was predominantly one-family, while the other side had a mixture of two-family "flats," as they were called, and more modest single- families. To put it simply, the rich lived on one side, the middle class the other. Gilmore Village, also in South Utica, was a public housing project isolated across the railroad tracks that ran through the southern end of the middle-class area.

South Utica was the home of the professional class, the doctors and lawyers and the top executives and middle managers of companies such as GE and Bendix. The owners of successful retail stores also lived there in the Proctor Boulevard and Ridgewood sections.

South Utica was all-white, with a large Irish Catholic population. Our Lady of Lourdes Church and its school formed the core of most Irish Catholic life in the city. Virtually all of Utica's Jewish population also lived in this section, although the primary temple, Beth-El was closer to the city center.

Wankel Field was home to the South Utica Little and Babe Ruth Leagues and also had a city playground and a small wading pool. Between Wankel and Murnane fields, at the other end of the neighborhood, there was an abundance of baseball fields and organized playground activities.

"Uptown" was the small commercial area serving the South End. Some of the businesses drew a larger base of consumers. King Cole ice cream and Jeans' Beans, a fish food takeout operation, were citywide attractions. Fish-only Friday customers at Jeans' Beans extended far out the door in long lines all day. The standard Friday Catholic meal was fried fish, French fries and beans. People did not eat out anywhere near as frequently as today. The Grand Union Super Market shopping center was just being developed. Noonan's' liquor store and the White Tower anchored the end of that commercial section along Genesee. All of these places were popular. The White Tower small hamburger with tiny onion pieces and ketchup was found here, and at its always-busy downtown location. The Uptown Theater was a South Utica movie destination.

A couple of small grocery stores like Andy's and Shultz's on Melrose served neighborhood needs, as did Pashayan's on Roosevelt. Many still stuck to the smaller grocery stores out of a sense of neighborhood loyalty and convenience. Credit was extended to regular customers. You paid by the week, or further out, depending on what the owner would grant. Remember, credit cards were in their national infancy and nearly nonexistent in Utica. Payment by check was also not widely accepted. Commercial transactions in the city, particularly in the neighborhoods, were still largely done with cash, or a handshake.

By and large, people lived, played, worshiped, shopped, and were educated within their neighborhoods. Kids played outdoors most of the time, on the playgrounds and in the empty lots, where they "captured the flag" or made their own ball fields. No one stayed inside.

You played in the streets, or in driveways shooting hoops, and sat on the steps of neighborhood stores drinking Ma's Root Beer, Orange Crush or Coke. A nickel Popsicle or Fudgesicle was a common treat.

Utica residents were, in general, inwardly directed. Most stayed within their neighborhood comfort zones, which were ethnic in nature. It was not that easy or common to travel even within the city. Some did not own cars. It was rare for a family to own two.

As a kid, you rode bikes but rarely, if ever, crossed neighborhood boundaries. Your best friends lived in your neighborhood. Visits between neighborhoods, for the most part, involved family functions or weekly drop-ins.

Professionals and merchants, to a great extent, worked in the office buildings and stores downtown, including the big department stores. Most mothers were stay-at-home, at least until kids went to high school. This meant that parents were always around. Neighborhood life was vibrant, intimate and fun. It seemed like everyone knew each other, all felt safe, and all respected their neighbors and neighborhood property.

It was really by bus, walking, or auto that the city came together, congregating in one place, the downtown. On weekends in particular, most "went Downtown." Utica became one in its vibrant center, where all major shopping, entertainment, professional business such as legal services, and government took place. Throw in some illegal bookmaking and the mosaic was complete. Downtown Utica sizzled with commerce, government, fun, good will, and a dose of sin.

Downtown

Think of a miniature version of Fifth Avenue and you'll understand downtown Utica in the '50s. Sidewalks were jammed with people walking from store to store to shop, eat, get their hair done, visit a lawyer, go to a movie, make a bet with a bookie, or see some live entertainment.

My fondest memories of downtown Utica as a young kid are of the Saturday trips with my dad. I always got to pick out an assortment of classic and Blackhawk comic books at a store on Lafayette Street that sold them at cut-rate prices with the front covers torn off. We always ended the excursion with hot fudge sundaes at Woolworth's. They were one scoop of vanilla with hot, very thick fudge sauce poured on top. To this day, they were the best hot fudge sundaes I ever had.

On Saturdays from morning to the dinner hours, the most alive place to be was "the busy corner," where Genesee and Bleecker met. Shoppers, strollers, moviegoers, downtown employees, people having lunch, cops, crooks, whites and blacks, you name it: all came downtown. It was fun, prosperous and full of history and interesting characters and events. Even the smells of the downtown food were fabulous.

One could walk the entire stretch of Genesee Street, from the Boston Store on the north side of Bleecker as far south as the Stanley Theater, and not be offered shopping, eating and entertainment choices. Genesee, packed with people, was indeed a smaller version of Fifth Avenue.

There were five major department stores: the Boston Store, Woolworth's, Neisner's, Kresge, and JB Wells, within two and a half blocks of each other. Berger's, a department store owned by a local family, was just a couple of blocks east on Lafayette Street. Many locally owned specialty shops were jammed into Genesee or spread east and west along Bleecker, Lafayette and Columbia. Four separate movie theaters and a couple of nightclubs provided entertainment. Everyone, and I mean everyone, took their kids to sit on Santa's lap at the Boston Store to present their Christmas lists. In all seasons, the smell of the roasted nuts at the Peanut Shop at the point of Washington and Genesee was irresistible.

Beauty shops, as hair salons were called in those days, saw customers ranging from the richest ladies from South Utica to the prostitutes of the West Utica houses of ill repute. Bookies flourished, all known and protected by the police. Visiting mobsters from New York City walked the streets with local relatives and associates.

One Saturday while on our usual downtown excursion, my father stopped at a locally owned store to say hello to one of his many downtown friends. While we were there, two cops pulled up and the store owner ran out with a couple of boxes of shoes. He expressed hope that they were the correct sizes. A few years later, it dawned on me that he was probably one of my father's bookies and that the cops were accepting look-the-other-way graft. Downtown was a power center on several layers, and the layer of corruption was not very hidden.

Top-level prostitutes sashayed around, had their hair done, ate out and were not shy about talking openly of their trade.

Downtown was also home to the Elefante controlled power structure operating within City Hall on Genesee, the Water Board on Washington Street, and the County Court House. The beauty of the city hall, an architectural gem, was dampened by the politics it housed.

Your lawyer worked in the First National Bank building, you deposited money in downtown banks, and you shot baskets and swam at the YMCA or the Knights of Columbus and could worship at several churches in or around the center of downtown.

You met friends, talked to the cops directing traffic at Busy Corner, took your kids clothes shopping, had your hair done or cut, ate lunch at an in-store restaurant, or grabbed a hamburg at the White Tower. A movie date, for those of all ages, could be at one of the four theaters where the major films were shown. The Stanley was home to an outstanding menu of live performances. As a little kid I was treated to Roy Rogers, Gene Autry, and their horses on the stage there. One of the horses could count by tapping his front hoof. Both cowboys were early TV stars and big movie draws. The Stanley was jammed with kids for both.

The theater was "the" major event center for live shows and movies since its opening in 1928. Its architecture was stunning. My father worked as an usher there in the early days including during part of the Depression.

There were even shoe departments and shoe stores aplenty, although in 1950 you had only two sneaker choices, Keds and Converse. A young man bought his first suit or sport jacket downtown. A tux for a prom would most likely be rented at Vitullo's, located on Hopper, a couple of blocks off the main drag.

As the shopper walked, shopped or ate, many eastern European languages were heard, spoken by those who immigrated to the city in the '20s and '30s. Shopping, hotels and services were an integrated racial picture, not seen in the all-white neighborhoods. Some residents first saw black people on a trip downtown.

The Hotel Utica was famous throughout the state and beyond, and the Pershing Hotel on the east side of Genesee a couple of blocks away from the "Busy Corner" was not far behind in style and grace. The top barbers worked in the hotels and trimmed the hair of many visiting celebrities, sports figures and politicians. There were no major motels, either in or outside of the city.

As celebrated in the Petula Clark song, downtown was the center of action for the city. In Utica's case it was the regional commercial and entertainment hub. For a taste of full city life, there was only one place to go, Downtown!

CHAPTER 3

The Early Years

The Personal Tale
Our First Stop

We moved to South Utica as I was about to enter second grade. Our large twin house on Prospect Street had been shared, as I've said, with Uncle Walt and his family. My parents Irene and Pete, my older sister Bernadette and I, lived in one half; Uncle Walt, his wife and their three children in the other. The arrangement was awkward from the start, since even though the men worked and invested together, the families were not at all close.

We attended John F. Hughes School, a short walk down the hill. Most kids in Utica walked to their neighborhood school. There were no city school buses for any city school. Many of the school's teachers also lived close enough to walk to their jobs. Students often met their teachers on the way to school.

As previously noted, South Utica was the wealthiest section of the city. Hughes had the children of the wealthy, particularly the non-Catholics, and many middle-class kids from what was called, "the other side" of Genesee. Most Catholic children of grade-school age attended the church school, Lourdes. If there was such a thing as "the poor" in South Utica, the public housing of Gilmore Village was it.

Gilmore was not, though, occupied by the poor as we know public housing residents today. Many units had war veteran families,
including widows of soldiers. Most families there were lower middle-class. Political connections did not hurt in landing an apartment
in Gilmore. Rent was low as in all subsidized housing. At Hughes,
"Village kids" tended to be looked down on by teachers and the more
well-off students.

One of my family members worked there. Public-housing jobs were
patronage jobs. The political ties of my father and uncle delivered a
job to their sister, Florence. She filled a bookkeeper's slot.

Florence always claimed that she was forced to leave her job, and the
city, as part of a cover-up of embezzlement at Gilmore. It was rumored
that she was forced out of town to avoid testifying in an impending investigation. Nothing ever came of it, but she did not return to Utica for
26 years. If the rumors were true, everything was squashed. It was hard
to fathom what really happened with Florence, but her story was sure
dramatic and not hard to believe given Utica's politics. I often wondered if she was part of the embezzlement scheme or just witness to it?

Hughes had no black kids and just a smattering of students with Italian
and Polish backgrounds. It was overwhelmingly Anglo, although with
a large number of Jewish students.

The principal was Jared Howland, a very nice guy who looked much
like a prep school headmaster. The teachers were mainly women,
some married but most not. I recall three men teachers: Mr. Fletcher,
Mr. Stewart and Mr. Hodinger, all of whom taught there in the latter
part of the decade. The faculty was highly competent, and strict.

No dress code was enforced, since there was no need to have one.
Again, dress at the time was relatively formal. There were no shorts,
no jeans, no T-shirts, no flip-flops, and no short skirts. We boys generally wore khaki pants and shirts that were more dress than casual.

Disciplinary problems were few. If you misbehaved, you were immediately sent to the principal's office, smacked, or so deeply verbally
embarrassed by your teacher that you carefully watched your behavior. The public school teachers were not that different in sternness
from the nuns at "St. Stan's." I never heard or saw a parent complain
about it. Teachers were in control. Of course, some behavior problems occurred, but they were few and far between. There was little
to no classroom disruption. One year a friend of mine, Ivor Surridge,
was caught smoking a cigar on the playground. The Hughes earth
shook.

The school had a hierarchy, set not only by economic circumstance
and brain power but also by the preferences of teachers who favored
a select few over the many. Wasp and wealthy Jewish students were
favored over the minority of Italian and Polish kids. At least, I and
others I knew strongly sensed this mild type of discrimination. Those
of us with Polish or Italian last names felt the need to work harder to
win the teachers' favor.

Although we of the middle class did feel a bit slighted by the teachers,
most students got along. I can recall only one incident in which an
anti-Polish slur was thrown in my face by another student. Many of us
"minorities" excelled in academics and sports. But on the downside,
the school's atmosphere—school life—was dimmer for students with
less money, less talent, and long last names.

The small representation of the two largest ethnic groups in the city,
Italians and Poles, at Hughes was not completely due to money.
Ethnic groups still chose to live together in older neighborhood clus-
ters. Since the Italians remained congregated in East Utica and the
Poles in West, kids went to neighborhood schools at which their eth-
nic group was a majority.

Roman Catholics, by far the largest religious group in Utica, were underrepresented at Hughes for another reason in addition to the ethnic residential patterns: Parents' desire to send their children to Our Lady of Lourdes.

Our neighborhood boys' gang leader was Dave Shaw, not surprisingly the toughest kid on the block. He and his family lived near us. Mrs. Shaw was a Cub Scout den mother. I went to one meeting, at which we carved animals out of soap. That was it for me. Another recollection is one of taking a piano lesson at our house while the guys stood on the porch in front of the window making fun of me.

Like most young boys, we passed much of our winter outdoor time throwing snowballs at cars and each other and playing "war" in the summer. War usually ended in an argument over who won. A snowball incident I never forgot occurred when a few of us were pelting cars driving by. I hit one with an open window. The driver caught it on the side of his head. He slammed on the brakes, jumped out and came after us. I completely froze, my legs could not move, and I was terrified. He came up to me in a rage, took a look at my almost-crying face, and just gave me a lecture. That was the last snowball I ever threw at a car. After the guy drove off, my friends reappeared in complete laughter while making fun of my "freezing up."

Not too long after moving to Prospect, we kids were told that we were leaving the house shared with Uncle Walt. It was a complete shock to my sister and me. My dad and my uncle had a falling-out, which ended their business relationship and made it impossible for the two families to coexist in the same house.

We were not given a reason for the falling-out. The story we were eventually told was that the two wives disliked each other and that this caused the residential split. I suspect the actual reason for the break between my father and uncle had more to do with money. Most family breakups do.

There is one aspect of our family and residential dispute that truly merits the saying "Life is sure a small world" in Utica. We were served with a formal eviction notice. It was served on behalf of the county sheriff by a guy named Stanley Powroznik. My wonderful wife is the former Christine Powroznik, Stanley's daughter! As Stan and my parents recalled the coincidence decades later, we all shook our heads in amazement. My parents and Stan shared a warm relationship before their respective passing. But the same cannot be said for the brothers.

My father and Walter never spoke to each other after we left Prospect Street. While both were alive, they handled their family of brothers and sisters in Utica as Michael and Fredo did in Godfather 2; they scheduled visits separately, knowing when the other was to visit in order to avoid crossing paths.

I have carried some guilt around for what I thought was a matter of honoring my father by never attempting to see, or speak with, my uncle. I also recall seeing him on occasions and avoiding him. When I learned of his passing, I was ashamed of myself for not at least being respectful enough to have said: "Hello, how are you?"

The Move to Parkside

I was eight years old when we moved to a house on Parkside Court, not far from Prospect. It was a relatively small house at the point where Parkside and Butterfield Avenue intersect. I loved the neighborhood. Across the street on the Butterfield side was a large area of woods and a makeshift baseball field. On the Bradford side were Hartnett's grocery store and another vacant lot. Today it is part of the Price Chopper center. That lot was where we played capture the flag—and where an older, rough bunch from Butterfield had a hut in which they drank beer and looked at dirty magazines. A bunch of us snuck in one day and spied the empty beer bottles and magazines. We were scared to death for fear of being caught and scandalized by our first peek at a dirty magazine.

Many kids from Hughes lived in the neighborhood. I quickly befriended the Jacobson brothers, Steve and Jeff, Donny Gagnon and Johnny Cahill from Baker Avenue, just a few blocks away. Sports dominated neighborhood life for kids of all ages.

They came to play ball on the diamond across the street. Virtually all were older than I. At first, holding my glove, I watched from the curb at my house. I saw Bill Galle with the sweetest swing I had yet seen. There was Jerry Coon, Al and Ron Curtis, Sonny Schmidt, Danny Hartnett, sometimes the Bertlesman brothers, and a whole bunch of other guys—some in college, some in high school, and some from Hughes but older than I was.

I'll never forget my first game there. It was like a TV commercial. I was sitting in my usual curb spot and one of the big guys asked, "Hey, want to play?" They were short a player and needed one to have even sides. I did. That very first day I hit a triple. It was a grounder, right over third base that made it to the street and then rolled. It was a cheapie, but it broke the ice and got me into many of the daily games.

In the '50s, kids of all ages played and interacted together on sandlots and playgrounds with no adults, no organized leagues, no forced enforced rules, and no conflict most of the time. We grew up fast and learned the streets by playing in and around them. We had neighborhood heroes and villains, had to be ready to stand our ground if picked on, and had to be good enough to be picked for a team when sides were chosen. Although nothing was organized by adults, one father of a friend did play a huge role in introducing me to a sport I grew to love: basketball.

John Cahill's father was Lefty Cahill, whom my father played with and against when they were young men. Mr. Cahill was a wonderful guy who still enjoyed basketball and was a member of the Knights of Columbus on Genesee near downtown. He took John, sometimes others, and me to shoot hoops on a regular basis. I loved it so much that I hung a small hoop on my bedroom door and shot baskets with rolled-up socks, night after night.

My introduction to bicycles also occurred on Parkside. I recall my first solo trip in the road. I panicked, riding around a parked car while another car was passing, and wound up running up the back end of the parked vehicle. As it did for all boys that I knew growing up, the bike became like a horse to a cowboy. We rode it all over. Most of us quickly graduated to the three-speed, thin-tired bikes called English bikes and rode them for years. I came to love the freedom of the bike, riding in the fresh air, my baseball glove hanging on the handlebars, with not a care in the world.

Influencing the path to manhood for young boys in the 50's was the western movie genre, a unique slice of Americana that offered the image of the strong, brave and righteous man that youngsters dreamed of, assumed the role in daily play, and even dressed as, the cowboy. In my life and many of the lives of my friends, the journey from Saturday morning westerns at the Rialto in east Utica, to Gary "Coop" Cooper in High Noon, to John Wayne at his best, provided what I would call mentors to a code. These mythical illustrations, combined with fathers, sports figures, coaches and well known locals, shaped the image of what a real man was. TV played a key role. During the 1950's, westerns were by far the single most popular shows on television. There were over sixty during the decade. Most disappeared by the mid-60's. It could be argued that this entertainment change alone signaled a changing image of manhood.

As I grew older, my friendship with the Jacobson brothers exposed me to a sport I hadn't known except by hearing or reading about it: golf.

The Jacobson's dad, Sol, was one of the best golfers in the area and played a good deal at the Twin Ponds course in New York Mills. In those days, "the Mills" was the home of the golfer sharpies who played much better than they let on if they smelled a betting opportunity. Many were terrific players. When I got a few years older, I was occasionally asked to join Steve and Jeff to caddy for Mr. Jacobson and others in his foursome. He was a great golfer and played for what was, at the time, big money. Guys came in from all over to play and bet. Exchanging hundred-dollar bills, huge money in those days, was not unusual in those matches. The winners tipped well. The Utica area was a hotbed of great golfers, including Ed Furgol, the New York Mills native who won the U.S. Open in 1954. He learned his trade at Twin Ponds.

The Jacobsons were fun and kind people, my first second family. Sol was an insurance man and Mrs. Jacobson, Shirley, a phys-ed teacher in the public schools. Steve was the oldest child, Jeff next, and Joann the young sister. I hung out at their house all the time, as did other neighborhood kids. We were always welcomed. At times the welcome was strained like the time we destroyed every window in their garage during a snowball fight.

At night during the good weather, all the kids including some girls, like my sister Bernie, hung out on the porch of Hartnett's store drinking a soda, eating a candy bar, talking and laughing. As one of the youngest, I was quiet and sometimes the deserving butt of the jokes.

One Halloween, a bunch of the guy teens threw rotten tomatoes all over the street near our house and Hartnett's. The fathers of the neighborhood got together, rounded up the culprits, and made them wash off the street with brooms and buckets of water. Never again did those guys desecrate the neighborhood.

A major lesson of the neighborhood in those days was that every family became on occasion your family, your surrogate parents. They shared the responsibility of providing safety, comfort, and backup when necessary. No one worried about where their kids were, or who they were with.

The neighborhood even counted a local newscaster celebrity in its midst. His name was Dick Clark. He lived with his parents and worked at a local radio or TV station. Every time my father noticed him walking by, he'd say, "There goes the dumbest guy in Utica." Yes, it was *the* Dick Clark, the future icon of American Bandstand. Some dumb! The neighborhood also had ties with other future celebrities.

The Giglios, yet another wonderful family, lived on Storres Ave few blocks from our house. Ann Marie, a friend of mine who would be a lasting one though high school and beyond, was a cousin of Utica's Annette Funicello of '50s and early '60s Hollywood fame. Although TV, still relatively new, and the movies were not all that important to kids at the time, some programs were not to be missed.

The Lone Ranger was my favorite TV show as I was already outgrowing Howdy Doody. I loved to hear "Hi Ho Silver Away" and watch Tonto aid his Kemo Sabe as they vanquished the bad guys. Death Valley Days was also up there on the list. Since television was still pretty new, show and channel choices were limited. Although people were taken with TV, it was not watched for anywhere near as much time as people spent in front of it later.

Our favorite passions in addition to sports were marbles, Tops baseball cards, and chestnuts.

All early-'50s kids played marbles. Part of the allure was that we gambled with them. Odd or even? Guess right and you'd win the other guy's in his hand. Guess wrong and you'd owe him however many marbles he had. Various winner-take-all marble "shooting" contests were also invented and played. "Clearies," or clear marbles, were much desired and rarely used in the games. To us kids they glistened like gold.

Most boys collected baseball cards. A pack of Tops could be bought for a nickel. In it were a piece of bubble gum and five or six major leagues cards, with a player's picture on the front and his stats on the back. Getting a Mantle was rare; a Tommy Lasorda was frequent. I threw away more Tommy Lasorda cards than you could count. Who was to know that he would become one of the best and most famous managers of all time? And who was to know that the cards of top players would someday be worth a small fortune as collector's items? We took great pleasure in trading cards with kids all over school to gather the full rosters of our favorite teams.

Chestnuts were yet another form of entertainment. Lining many streets on our way to school were huge chestnut trees. The attraction of the green, prickly covers with shiny brown chestnuts inside was irresistible. The fallen ones were picked, others knocked off the trees by various methods. They were polished and collected, items like rings and necklaces were made out of them, and they were also thrown as weapons by warring boys. You could say the chestnuts were yet another form of entertainment.

Yo-yos were a national and local craze. Kids and many adults fell in love with it and the tricks that could be done. "Walk the dog" and "cat's cradle" were just two of many. Yo-yo tricksters appeared at stores to promote the latest design. The fad seems laughably quaint given today's video gadget fixation.

While we're on the topic of entertainment, more movies of the time come to mind. One Easter, at age eight, I went all alone to watch Quo Vadis, a Roman-vs.-Christian sword fighting epic, at the Uptown Theater with my chocolate Easter bunny wrapped in tin foil. Imagine an eight-year-old going to the movies alone today. The parents would be arrested.

We rarely went to movies as a family, and I never understood why. I now imagine, looking back, that my father hated the musicals that my mother loved and she disliked the kinds of movies that were to my father's taste. I was dragged kicking and screaming to The Great Caruso, Showboat, and An American in Paris, all at the Stanley, while my father took me to view his favorite, Robert Walker, in Strangers on the Train and Bogey in The African Queen. When he allowed me to wear my six-guns to see High Noon at the Oneida Theater in 1951, it would forever be the highlight of my childhood movie memories.

We did watch some TV as a family. Two shows in particular, Milton Berle and Jack Benny, were among our favorites. Ed Sullivan's variety show was also popular with us, and much of the viewing public. We also enjoyed the weekly Martin and Lewis show.

Part of life became work, not play. I became a first-time wage earner at a young age. Pat Comesky, our neighborhood paper boy, hired me to help deliver the afternoon/evening *Observer Dispatch*. In those days the city was served by two papers, the *Daily Press* in the morning and the OD in the late afternoon. I got paid a dime, which I always promptly spent on a piece of tomato pie at Jim's on Auburn Avenue. It was my first introduction to Utica tomato pie. Today's readers will be shocked to know that there were no pizza parlors, as I recall. One or more might have started by then in East Utica, but they were not citywide attractions.

But more than school work, more than tomato pie, more than anything else, sports continued to be my obsession.

The year, 1951, represented the start of baseball in my life and also began of one of the most significant decades in the sport's history nationally. Joe DiMaggio in his last year, Duke Snider already a star, and Mickey Mantle and Willie Mays in their rookie year all played in New York for the Yankees, Dodgers and Giants. They were the best center-fielders in the game and would be for years.

My father took me to a game at the Polo Grounds, the home of the Giants, to see a Giants-Brooklyn Dodgers game. Antonelli against Podres. There were Bobby Thomson, Don Mueller, Alvin Dark, Monte Irvin, Larry Jansen, and Mays for the Giants; Snider, Pee Wee Reese, Carl Furillo, Gil Hodges, Roy Campanella, Sal "the Barber" Maglie, and the most exciting player I ever saw, Jackie Robinson, for the Dodgers. The Giants won, but the Dodgers were still far ahead in first place in the National League. I came home a Giants fan.

By the end of the season in September, the Dodger lead of 13 games in August disappeared and the two teams faced each other in a three-game series to determine who would go to the World Series. In those days, games were played during the day, the World Series really was in October, and teachers and students listened to the games during class. Both leagues, American and National, had eight teams. There were no playoffs. Players smoked in the dugouts and did cigarette commercials on the radio and now TV. They also had to work in other jobs in the off-season to make ends meet. There were no contracts of even $100,000 and no free agency. World Series checks meant a good deal to the players' incomes.

I still recall coming home from school, running into the house, and being able to catch the final inning of the third game. In the bottom of the ninth, Bobby Thomson hit "The Shot Heard Round the World," the homer that won the game and the pennant for the Giants in one swing of the bat. They lost the Series to the Yankees, but that paled in importance compared with beating the Dodgers, their fiercest rival in baseball, in such dramatic fashion. The next nine years would be a glorious period for New York baseball arguably even greater than in the Ruth- Gehrig era.

It was unimaginable at the time that both the Dodgers and the Giants would leave New York within the decade. To many of my age who grew up as Dodger fans, the Dodgers would always be the Brooklyn Bums.

The '50s featured some of the greatest players and teams to ever play. Utica had two in the majors at the time, Hal White and Ted Lepcio. White played with the Tigers, Ted with the Red Sox. My father knew them both, had played against Hal when he was younger, and let Teddy, known as "Chubby," carry his glove to games in the old days. Lepcio was an East Utica Pole, and his sister was my mother's closest friend at St. Stan's and a bit later. I was to play both baseball and basketball against Hal White, Jr. in high school. He was a good athlete and a chip off the old block in terms of niceness. The professional players of the '50s had no huge egos or chips on their shoulders. They were not high earners, and virtually all needed off-season jobs to make ends meet.

Race was still an issue. Although Jackie Robinson broke the color line in the late '40s, discrimination remained strong in the '50s. It nearly disappeared, though, by the end of the decade. Some teams, such as the Boston Red Sox, were slow to integrate and most had unwritten quotas that limited the number of blacks. However, public trash talk and discrimination from the stands were coming to an end.

In his youth, my father was a terrific athlete himself, even playing baseball for a spell in the minors. Unfortunately, he also loved to bet on sports. He played better than he bet, and did not limit his habit to baseball. Within two years after we moved there, we lost the house on Parkside and once again had to move. Looking back on things as I matured, I realized why he got so heated and excited while listening to ball games or watching boxing on TV.

The reader might ask how anyone did all that betting. Was not gambling illegal? There were no OTBs, Indian casinos or government lotteries. What the city did have was a bookie on every block. Gambling was one of the most lucrative businesses in Utica, which was wide open to it. In every plant, for example, you could find the "house bet taker." I worked at one business in the '60s in which the union head was also the onsite bookie rep. If management knew what was going on at all, they turned their backs and looked at it as something that was good for employee relations.

My mother worked hard all the time and became the family's dependable bread earner as assistant manager and then manager of the Boston Store Beauty Salon. She was to work there for nearly 50 years.

My father Pete was a licensed private investigator who had clients on a hit-and-miss basis. I once found his .45 hidden in our basement. He had no office and operated basically out of the house. He was also a city employee, in the Department of Public Works. He had a title but was rarely there, one of many, with no-show, padded-payroll jobs common to Utica politics and government. As a political operative of Denny O'Dowd, West Utica's Democratic boss, my dad had that perk too, like others who could muster votes or financial contributions for the Democratic machine. I understood that situation at a young age, since we worried when headlines appeared in the *Daily Press* about padded payroll jobs and mentioned a "private investigator" as one example. My father was never named, and investigations never moved forward. But the crusading drumbeat of the Utica newspaper never stopped beating. By 1958, the political corruption issue would come to a head.

My memories of Parkside are happy ones. On Fridays we watched The Big Story crime show and the Gillet Friday Night Fights of great boxing matches. Families and friends were close both literally and figuratively. Friends like Jeff and Steve Jacobson were people I still count as lifetime friends. No one made a big deal about having money. All took pride in the neighborhood while making sure it was safe for us kids and well- kept. Weekly religious services were the norm for most families, including ours. Religious customs from earlier times, earlier generations were continued.

In 2017, my wife and I went to a very moving Holy Thursday Mass as part of our Easter observance. The priest saying the Mass, Father Arthur, was a wonderful young man who is highly inspirational, to say the least. A Polish immigrant and now a U.S. citizen, he mentioned "visiting churches" in his homily. I'm pretty sure not many of the people listening knew what he meant. We did.

Catholics in Utica in the '50s celebrated Holy Thursday with the custom of visiting churches. Families got all dressed up and stopped by a minimum of five churches to say a prayer at each. The streets of Utica teemed with people walking into and out of neighborhood churches. It was a moving and unifying custom that has disappeared in tandem with the decline in church attendance.

The Parkside house was sold. We then moved into a second-story flat on Cornwall Avenue, a street between Sunset and Roosevelt, and a stone's throw from Our Lady of Lourdes church and school. My parents were never to own a house again. My mother refused to take a chance on owning another one, despite both the financial advantage of the investment and the fact that her husband rid himself of the gambling itch. They were happy renters for the rest of their lives.

CHAPTER 4

Mid-Decade

Cornwall

When we moved to Cornwall Ave., Patti Page was singing, "How Much Is That Doggie in the Window," Ike was ending the Korean War, Boyd Golder was still Mayor of Utica, and Rufie the power behind the throne. The music was corny, the Yankees were the best, the Syracuse Nationals part of the early days of the NBA, and Michigan State the top college football team. Believe it or not, the Detroit Lions ruled pro football.

The new neighborhood seemed full of life and kids, school started to be interesting, and sports were growing even more important to me. Kids of all ages jammed the streets; Riley's, McCabes, Sullivans, Middaughs, Bernsteins and the big guy on the block, Jim Klein.

The city was a hotbed of sports, ranging from great semi-pro baseball and basketball Leagues, to great high school football, to top-flight golfers teeing up at Twin Ponds in "the Mills" to outstanding tennis at the Parkway Courts. Top-notch college football was nearby at Colgate and Syracuse. Utica College of Syracuse University was still downtown, but efforts to develop a new campus were in the early stages of thoughts and discussions. Jobs were plentiful and the downtown full of hustle and bustle.

The Elefante/Golder style of governing was to concentrate on the basics. That meant excellent services like street paving and cleaning, plenty of law enforcement in the neighborhoods, good maintenance of the wonderful park system the city was blessed with, and constructing new public buildings. There was a saying that the "Rufie formula" was a new public building every election year.

For example, the Utica Memorial Auditorium was announced as a new project in 1957, a local election year. According to the street buzz, its site was selected as a political payoff. It was owned by some of Rufie's businessmen supporters. That was never proven, but it became part of the folklore of Elefante bossism, in which most major decisions were corrupt in one way or another. Corrupt or not, the city was physically attractive, even stunning in some unique ways.

Utica's founding families left a huge, gorgeous park system and open space that ran along the city's eastern border from the Memorial Parkway to the end of Culver Avenue. That system included the municipal Robert Trent Jones golf course, which opened for play in 1927. On the Oneida Street border, a solid bank of public tennis courts was available along with an ice skating rink and modest ski area.

Utica had no slums by today's standards. The good city services helped to maintain decent neighborhoods, but the true reason for such stability was the pride citizens took in their homes and neighborhoods Houses were kept freshly painted, lawns were cut, and littering was unknown. Income had little to do with the standards by which you kept your neighborhood and house pristine. Pride and a sense of responsibility did. A neighbor who allowed his place to become run-down heard about it directly from the neighbors. These standards led to growth in property values and a strong housing demand prompted by interest in remaining a city resident while moving up the economic ladder.

The neighborhood of which Cornwall was part extended from Barton to Cornwall to Dryden to Melrose. All of those streets were bordered by Sunset and Roosevelt. Fairfax, the street Cornwall became on the other side of Sunset, was part of the neighborhood, as was upper Melrose. It was a neighborhood loaded with kids, working parents from various walks of life, the nuns and priests of Lourdes, and a middle-class ethnic and religious mix. We kids of the neighborhood, particularly the boys, lived for sports.

I was starting to play a lot of basketball, which for me included riding a city bus every Saturday morning to play in a young kids' league run by Stan Zybiak at the downtown YMCA. Stan was an old friend of my fathers who was active in youth sports at the Y and youth tennis at the Parkway. He was a dedicated coach for us youngsters. He was also as nice a man as could be found.

The Jacobsons had moved from Bradford Avenue to a house on the Parkway close to Genesee. They had a hoop on their garage, and for the next couple of years I would walk back and forth from Cornwall to their house to play. I still shiver at the many times I walked home freezing during the winter, sneakers wet and cold, while still sweating from the driveway games. Like most kids who shoot hoops, we were oblivious to everything else including snow, shoveling off the driveway and the cold.

My first memorable encounter in the neighborhood occurred when I was walking from our home, along Fairfax to Andy's Superette, a small store on upper Melrose. I noticed a tall figure shooting baskets in a driveway-garage hoop, then started walking in closer and saw that it was a short-haired girl. I later learned she was one of the many Denn kids, who lived next to Lourdes school. One of us shouted a challenge.

Legend has it that she beat me one-on-one. I don't think that is true, but I tell it that way myself. (Fiction is often a far better story to tell.) As I recall the actual game, I won by a basket or two. But she was good and extremely competitive, to say the least. Later, in high school, Sheila was to be my first real girlfriend. But at the time, we were just hanging on Fairfax with a group of kids, playing a whole bunch of different kinds of games day and night, ending the evening by sitting and goofing around on the Denn's porch. Mr. Denn wasn't around much as he worked a mid-day shift at the New York Central station downtown. Mrs. Denn was an absolute saint in addition to being one of the most stately, attractive women I have ever known. The family was as Catholic as Catholic could be. That likely explained its horde of kids!

Even though we now lived just half a block from Lourdes, my sister and I remained at Hughes. My mother's anti-parochial school attitude was set in stone.

To get from Cornwall to Hughes, you had to walk a kind of Lourdes gauntlet, the groups of kids arriving at the school. We heard catcalls daily, for the Hughes/Lourdes rivalry was fierce. I always tried to walk with some tough guys so I could be in a protective group. When the Lourdes kids saw one of them, Don Broccoli, coming they shut up.

In those days, we Catholic kids in public schools were allowed to leave early on certain days to attend religious instruction at Lourdes. The nuns viewed us as youngsters badly in need of salvation and were not all that friendly. We just enjoyed getting out of class early and comparing our experiences in school with those the Lourdes kids had to be going through. I was thankful for Hughes.

Life at Hughes

School was sure fun as the '50s moved along. There was little pressure except from some schoolyard bullies. A few others and I did, however, experience one change that, although we didn't realize it at the time, would become a problem not of our making.

LUCKY U, LUCKY US

It happened in the 4th grade. At that time, school terms were measured in half-years. Three other students and I were given the opportunity to skip a half-year thanks to our excellent grades and behavior. My mother considered the offer a matter of recognition and pride, and we accepted. One of my best friends, Stew Pratt, another one of the three, advanced as well. That meant we finished in the fall semester and would enter 5th grade in the second half of the school year. We became what were called "odd-term students." No one realized the future implications of graduating from high school in the winter rather than the normal early-summer graduation. That would turn out to be a curse to me and others, especially athletes. College scouts, for example, often lost sight of the off-termed players, who seemed to disappear from the high school teams.

My main classroom memories are of Mrs. Redmond in part of the 4th grade—one of the two best and nicest teachers I ever had—and my 6th grade teacher, the tough Mrs. Wagner. She walked up and down the aisles tugging the hair of the boys she thought were slackers. I always wore a very short crew cut, which frustrated her; she would smile and shake her head. She was actually a very nice lady and an excellent teacher who demanded that all work hard in class. Mrs. Wagner had tough rules of conduct and study, and she enforced them.

My school friends at the time were kids from the Proctor Boulevard/ Douglas Crescent area who were both in my class and lived close to my path home. In those days, you could take a shortcut from the Ballantyne Brae side of the school over a dirt road that led through the St. Elizabeth Hospital property. The kids who lived in the area also used that route and played in the back of the hospital property, where a huge mound of dirt from new construction was massed. We named it Mount Suribachi, where our flag was raised on Iwo Jima in the Pacific in World War II. We picked sides and fought to defend or capture the mountain with fierce winter snowball fights. Al Silverberg, David Parker, Stevie Wynn, Stew Pratt, the Nathans and many others spent virtually every winter day after school fighting for that hill!

I also spent a good deal of time at friends' houses. All had welcoming, hospitable parents. Of particular warmth were Steve Wynn's parents. You would be hard- pressed to meet a lady as nice as Mrs. Wynn and a man as interesting as Mr. Wynn. He was involved in the bingo business, which took him on the road quite a bit. I loved seeing and talking to him. Mrs. Wynn always welcomed Steve's friends. Either the Wynns or the Parkers had an old slot machine in the basement which we fooled around with. Steve now resides in a very different neighborhood filled with slots and other games.

As I started to play more sports—a lot of sports—my friendships shifted. The hectic, competitive sports scene was on the other side of Genesee.

Street Ball

Bill Benz, who lived at Dryden and Roosevelt, was the neighborhood's sports impresario. He invented and played more games than you could count on two hands. We played different variations of ball in the street, in the empty lots, and in the house when it rained. Whiffle ball, football, cotton ball, tennis ball, any kind of ball: we played it. Two or four of us even played tennis ball automatics off the house stairs. David Berkeley, Tom Kent, Mike Brown, and others from Melrose often played. Mike Sewell, Benz, and some kids from Gilmore Village like John Prendergast joined in. We were never short of players.

The relationships formed then were to continue, with many, through high school as I played both with and against my neighborhood pals.

Just about any street game activity, anywhere in the neighborhood, ended with a soda and ice cream at Andy's on Melrose. I can still taste the Ma's Root Beer or orange crush and the "cho-cho bars," which were chocolate-covered ice cream on a stick that was positively addictive. But not all thoughts of young boys centered on sports and treats.

"Benzy" and I somehow found out that one of his lady neighbors loved to play poker. On rainy days once in a while, we would sneak into her house and play for pennies as her kid slept. I guess she was one of the bored 1950s housewives people wrote novels about. She was awfully nice—and pure as Ivory soap, although this young man's mind was not. She just liked poker.

That was not the only one of my older-woman fantasies. When I took over a newspaper route in the 7th grade, I made my collections in the evening. One of my customers was a bombshell of a lady, built like Sophia Loren. Her husband worked a night shift, so she was the one who usually answered the door when I came collecting. More often than not, she wore a negligee that was pretty revealing. She made for some sinful thoughts. My field of dreams was expanding.

The older a ball player became, the larger the area in which he hunted games. Not many houses had basketball hoops. In addition to the Jacobson home, the place to play was at Johnny Ryan's on Proctor Boulevard. The Ryans had a huge driveway with a nifty free-standing basket. John, who was a Catholic schoolkid, and some of his buddies like Jerry Friel regularly came over to play, as did neighbor Ivor Surridge and others. But the biggest activity and thrill for kids in South Utica was not shooting driveway baskets or playing street ball. It was playing Little League Baseball.

South Utica Little League

The South Utica Little League was a very big deal to the players, the adults who ran it, the coaches, and the parents. It featured the cream of the crop of the city's very good young baseball player and was enthusiastically embraced by many residents from all over South Utica—not league-affiliated people, but fans. It seemed that all of Utica was tuned in to Little League. Stands were jammed all over the city.

Utica was always a good baseball town. The Utica Blue Sox, the Phillies' Class A affiliate, had featured some of the 1950 Whiz Kids, National League pennant winners, like Richie Ashburn, Stan Lapotta and Granny Hammer. Their great pitcher Jim Konstanty, the 1950 World Series Most Valuable Player was from nearby Oneonta). Even before the franchise started in 1946 (it folded in 1950), great baseball was played in the city and many excellent touring teams streamed through to play Utica's best. The competition was very intense on any level, and Little League was no exception.

Although the age qualification was 8 to 12, not many made it at eight. If you made it at eight or nine, you sat the bench. There was no requirement to let everyone play. Skill not age determined if a kid played or sat the bench. And, there were no lesser leagues as there are today. There were no travel teams. There were no sports camps. Little League was it.

I had made a team at age nine. We were the King Cole's team. That was rich, since King Cole's was where everyone went for ice cream after a game, a practice, or pickup game of any sort, even with your family on a hot night. What a great sponsor! At times, when we won a big game, our coaches Mr. Humphries and Mr. Obernesser would meet us there for a free ice cream treat. Playing for an ice cream sponsor sure beat playing for Pulver Roofing. Their players didn't get, or want, a shingle after a win.

Many on my team were already friends. Others would become and stay friends for life. Some parents took us places to share family activities like a picnic and a swim at Power Dam, a local swimming area on a hill at Upper Higby Rd. and Mohawk Street. Most parents came to all of the games. Contrary to most of what's often said about Little League parents, I recall no fights, arguments or petty incidents among ours. Times were different, and respect was a shown to all.

The games were played at Wankel Field. I still remember walking up to the field for a game hearing "Rags to Riches" or "Cherry Pink and Apple Blossom Time" blaring on the loudspeaker, while getting all excited about the game to be played. The popcorn was popping and the hot dogs frying. Great smell. "Take me out to the ball game, take me out to the crowd ...." Little League was the beginning of the dream of making the Majors, the dream of many little boys.

Part of Wankel's excitement, appeal, and warm relationships stemmed from its location and the people who lived near it. The neighborhood was one of Lebanese- and Syrian-Americans, many related to each other, most with big families, who had kids playing in the League. Virtually all of the neighborhood was involved in one way or another. I still marvel at the crowds, and the old-timers standing along the fences and behind the team benches, watching and commenting on the games and cheering on good play.

I have the fondest memories of the Tomaselli, Tozzi, Massoud, Barkett, Joseph, Gozy and Nackley families who one way or another were around every game night. Chuck Tomaselli was a teammate of mine, and his dad was a great fan and an even greater guy. He often took us to Power Dam for a picnic and a swim. I still have a picture of Steve Wynn, another teammate, and me at Power Dam with me on Steve's shoulders. Yes, Steve Wynn of the Proctor Boulevard area bunch is *that* Steve Wynn, now a fixture of Las Vegas fame and fortune. My father often joked that Steve, as a baseball player, "had two left feet." What neither he nor anyone at the time would ever have imagined is that Steve would become a billionaire and world-famous casino developer. As with his assessment of Dick Clark, my father obviously had limited vision for where the real talent lay. Steve may not have hit well in Little League, but he sure hit it big in Las Vegas.

Over the years I played, I had many friends on my team and throughout the league. I continued to meet many of them as friends, teammates or competitors in years to come.

King Cole had some excellent players such as Les Lewis, Donnie English, Johnny Green, Mike Brown and a few others. Several became high school and college players. Our teams were competitive, but not the League's best.

The league's dynasty was held by the Scheidelman's team, coached by Frank Boden. They were the Yankees of South Utica Little League. In those years, guys like Mike Evans, Phil Obernesser, Frank Donalty and a whole string of strong players led them. In '55, my final year, they featured ace pitcher John Prendergast, Tom Khoury—the best catcher around and several other excellent players like Ray Schaedler and Gary Madia.

In 1955, Prendergast and I were selected as the #1 and #2 pitchers of the All Star team. The team was loaded with talent and carried with it high hopes for tournament play.

We probably dreamed of playing in Williamsport, Pennsylvania, the site of the Little League World Series but never discussed it with each other. Our coaches, Frank Boden and Jack Barkett, never mentioned it. We all knew we had a really great team, but we just played game by game. And we kept winning.

Our main opposition as we competed to advance beyond the Utica area and region came from an equally good West Utica team. Guys like Foxenberg, Krumm, Saville, Prymas, Gilberti and Wiklacz could play. Many would go on to play in high school, some against and some with me. No thanks to me, we beat the west enders, 4-3. I got knocked out of the box early. Pete Palewski saved our bacon pitching in reserve while Prendergast, Schaedler, Khoury and Dickie Tuttle drove in enough runs to squeak out the win. Even though we won, I was crushed getting crushed.

As we kept winning, we earned a trip to the state tournament in Scotia. We started to realize that it was a big deal to the city and our neighborhood. We were getting press ink and moving closer to the big prize, a trip to the Little League World Series. We started to think of a dream coming true, and as we did, the pressure grew. Our first opponent in Scotia was the team from Schenectady who were the defending Little League World Champions! And they had many of those same players.

I pitched the game, which we won, 4-1. I recall two things about it. Mike Brown made a great catch in right field, to end the game with guys on base. Our coaches took us that night to a local TV station to watch the report on the game. (I guess motels did not have TVs in their rooms then.) I was really pumped with the idea that I would be cited on TV! As we watched the newscast, the game report came on and I was referred to as Roger Patucci. They butchered "Potocki" and made an Italian out of a Pole. My teammates hooted and hollered while I turned red and was truly deflated. But we had one game left before we advanced to the Northeast regionals, so "Patucci" was not important. Since we'd beaten a team that had won it all the previous season, why couldn't we do that ourselves? Why not us? We looked ahead a bit too far.

When we saw our opponents from Glens Falls, especially their pitcher, I think our attitude was that we had a sure win. Their hurler was a very small, skinny kid going up against our ace, John Prendergast, who was a dynamite pitcher. I don't think any of us even considered losing that game a possibility.

The little kid had a wicked curve that no one could touch. And his team could not touch John. We went into the last inning tied 0-0. In their half of the inning, a kid lofted a long fly to left field that looked catchable. Our left fielder got his glove on it and backed into the wall. The ball fell out of his glove, over the fence. We lost 1-0. We were so shocked that I don't recall anyone saying a word on the long bus ride home. One or two guys softly cried. The dream ended so suddenly. But bounce back we did.

Many of us were out playing pickup at Wankel the following week. I think to this day, those of us who played there through those young years feel lucky. We had a lot of friends who remained friends, even many from other leagues. My good friends like Stew Pratt, who was not a good hitter but hit me like he owned me, Chuck Tomeselli, Les Lewis, Mike Brown, Gary Madia, Tom Khoury, and many others were examples of that, and in some cases future teammates. And other kids, like Bart Gorman and Harvey Cramer, were a good deal of fun to play with.

These boys stayed friends and school mates of each other as we eventually went on to high school and college. Some remained lifetime friends of mine. They included players from other parts of the city. South Utica Little League enriched the lives of a countless number of young kids in this way and by expanding our horizons of the city.

Our coaches did not coach well technically, by today's standards, but took very good care of us and taught us some very valuable lessons of life. Many older assistant coaches like Jim and Bill Fullem, Jim Klein, and others were ball breakers, but mentors as well. I looked up to Bill Fullem as a hero of sorts. The hyper parents of today who yell, scream, fight, and fire coaches did not exist in the 1950s. As many of us grew older, we always shared a good word and greeting with coaches Frank Boden, Jack Barkett, Ken Humphries and others.

A mention of Judy Noonan is warranted whenever the '50s South Utica Little League comes up. Judy was the official scorekeeper and the league's number-one fan for years. Although I still, 62 years later, think our catcher Johnny Gozy made an error that Judy scored as a hit, thus robbing me of a no-hitter, I vividly recall her dedication to a game that girls in those days were not allowed to play.

Of course, as with all organized activities involving kids, the experience did trigger negative pressures, rivalries, and jealousies. I often feared failure, and once in a while resented what I viewed as favoritism shown to others. As I grew older and looked back, I came to realize that the South Utica Little League provided lessons in finishing what you start, competition, teamwork, and even failure that prepared us for later life. As I watched my kids and grandkids grow up, I concluded that such lessons back in '55 were much more productive for us than the modern youth-sports world.

Important to our lives as the Little League experience was, the larger world of the country, and the city, was far more so.

The Real World at the Time

The Salk vaccine, which would eradicate polio, was approved in 1955 as my Little League experience ended. . A singer named Elvis opened at concerts of Bill Haley and the Comets, of "Shake Rattle and Roll" fame. North and South Vietnam would split and start fighting, Albert Anastasia was tried for tax evasion, and the Mickey Mouse Club made its TV debut. Utica became a key player as a world technological center when its General Electric division plant made national headlines as the developer of the most advanced radar system to date. And a little lady named Rosa Parks would not give up her bus seat in Montgomery, Alabama.

The Utica Parkway recreation area hosted a religious ceremony on May Day to honor Mary and St. Joseph. When an outdoor mass was held at the city band shell, the attendance was 20,000! The largest religious service in the city's history, it clearly demonstrated the extent to which religion was a pillar of the Utica community.

OLOL

In South Utica, the Irish-Catholic part of the city, Our Lady of Lourdes parish was the city's largest, richest, and most dominant Catholic institution. It was sometimes an uncomfortable place for a Polish-American Catholic boy who attended public school.

At the top of the Lourdes hierarchy was Father Collins. He was a wee bit of a man who sat behind the wheel of a big, black, luxurious Cadillac. He wielded immense influence. In the parish, he directed at least three other priests. Masses were held in the small church on Genesee, with one large Sunday morning Mass in the big school auditorium. Held at 11:30, it was very popular. Late morning and no kneeling were a tough combo to beat. But the fire-and-brimstone preaching of Father Corbett warning, "No good happens after midnight" still occupies my memory. He sure did not preach the message of love.

The school was run by nuns of the Sisters of Charity, dressed in their habits complete with "wings." They taught all classes except gym.

The church was part of my morning paper route. The first time I rang the bell to collect money from the rectory, the housekeeper informed me that I had to meet Father Collins, or better yet, he had to meet me. He was such an imposing man, in so many ways, that I shook with nervousness.

I met him privately in a small room. He kept referring to me as a "Pole" and questioned why I went to public school, since I was Catholic and lived but a stone's throw from Lourdes. All I recall was that I was both blushing and stammering from being asked about something I had no control over. I walked out with the money and did not care if I never spoke to the good father again.

I carried around, for some time, the idea that I was both looked down upon by the Lourdes Irish and in some instances discriminated against because I was an outsider. It is likely that many people of all ages in Utica in the '50s still had the baggage of different ethnic perceptions. Terms like "dumb Polack," "crooked Italians," and "drunken Irish" were used fairly frequently. But ethnic bias and differences aside, God did show himself in 1955. The Dodgers finally beat the Yankees! All in all, it was a very good year.

Goodbye Hughes

Walking up Proctor Boulevard one day in 1956, I heard "Heartbreak Hotel" blaring out of a house with an open window. But as I look back on that day, my strongest recollection is that kids, particularly the young girls of that time, were not blown away by Elvis. He and his hip- shaking were not a big deal in Utica. Although "Heartbreak Hotel" was #1 nationwide, the Platters songs "My Prayer" and "The Great Pretender" were more popular here. Dean Martin's "Memories Are Made of This" was not far behind. Elvis's second release, "Don't Be Cruel," was more popular locally than his first.

That year, "The Ten Commandments" was the most widely viewed movie nationwide and in Utica. It probably could not be made, as it was then, today. Jimmy Dean was an instant star, worshipped by the girls and "cool" to the guys. After "Rebel Without a Cause," a boy who was to be "in "had to wear a red nylon Jimmy Dean jacket. I did most of the time—and froze when it got cold. But young kids then, as they do now, chose "cool" over warmth and common sense.

In the 7th and 8th grades, things started to change for us as we sensed the differences between a small and a big school. What brought us the sense of difference was knowing and interacting with older, high school age kids. In my case, my sister was at Utica Free Academy and also because I followed high school sports. Looking back, I eventually realized the value of my years at Hughes.

Most important, I realized how good most of our teachers were. Miss Gill taught us solid English and Henrietta Lamour was a top-notch history teacher. We knew how to construct a sentence, could recite the Gettysburg Address, knew the Civil War battles, knew the role New York State played in the Revolution and Utica's early importance to the state and nation.

We boys also got the hint that girls were kind of exciting. My first school girlfriend, Kathy Nicholson, was a looker who was also smart. At that age, a girlfriend was someone you exchanged notes with in school and once in a while walked home after a school dance. I think we held hands, but that was it. I got very nervous and choked on any occasion when I might have grabbed a kiss.

Some of us also sought, and were given, responsibilities that exceeded our age. One was the safety patrol. What was that? It was 7th and 8th graders, wearing white belts and silver badges, directing younger kids at street crossings and "patrolling" the school playgrounds to help keep order. Today, taxpayers pay adults and teachers to do those tasks.

In the 8th grade, I became captain of the safety patrol. One of my first jobs was to recruit and assign my underlings. I had a brilliant idea. I recruited the two toughest kids in school, Donnie Broccoli and Ed Milewski, and assigned them playground patrol duty. It was a year of the most peaceful playground in Hughes's school history! Many teachers were aghast, but my strategy worked.

A good deal of my time and interest was still devoted to baseball and basketball. Hap Holehan was our coach. You could not ask for a nicer, gentler guy, and he instilled a high level of sportsmanship in his players. We had some very good players in both sports.

LUCKY U, LUCKY US

My friends, Jeff Jacobson, Rod Supiro, Mickey Nackley, Gary Madia, Dickie Tuttle, Luke Medici, and Dave Berkeley played one or both sports and were part of excellent teams. We shot ourselves in the foot, though, by losing both city championships in our final Hughes year.

When we played Roosevelt in the basketball showdown, they had a nice team, with Tony Adorino as their scoring star and Harold Hansen as their big guy. Our team was much deeper and therefore better. I was our point guard, even though I was already over six feet tall and one of the bigger guys on the court. My passing and outside shooting ability were well- suited to the guard positon.

I fell and broke my wrist halfway through the second half. I tried to play, but couldn't hold or shoot the ball with a bum right hand. We got nipped. The next day all the girls felt sorry for me and signed my plaster cast. Anytime I bump into someone who played in that game, from either side, they recall the wrist break. Players on all levels tend to keep vivid memories of key games. Older people remember them more, although probably less accurately.

In baseball, pitchers dominated. I was but one of many solid throwers. As a pitcher, you had to strike out a lot of guys to win, since fielding at the grade-school level was full of errors. One game, I fanned 18 out of 21 outs. Tony Adorino, Carl Graziadi, Doug Napp, and a kid named Leo Latore were all excellent pitchers. Latore, who pitched for Seymore, beat us in the 2-to-1 in the title game. Some people, like my catcher and our heavy hitter Mickey Nackley, who I now often see in church, still recall that game and that team. Losses in big games remain memories as long as, or longer than, wins on any rung of the sports ladder.

Win or lose, sports at Hughes led you to an outside world players would not have experienced that early in Utica life. In those days of self-contained neighborhoods and schools limited a grasp of a full city feel. As a player, especially playing basketball and baseball, you expanded your experiences and friendships throughout the city. Being recruited to play on all-star teams in various citywide tournaments expanded them further. One great annual event was the East Utica Boys Club basketball tournament. Several all-star teams from citywide roster mixes competed.

The Boys Club was located in the heart of East Utica, in a relic of a building. The gym was small and on the second floor. There was so little room under the basket on the street side of the gym that when you drove in to the basket, you felt like you might fall out the window! I do not recall details of the tourney, but do know that all of the top players in the grade-school league played in it. My team won it all, and I was named MVP. I found out about the award the day after the next game, in the lobby of the Stanley Theatre, buying popcorn before a Sunday movie. A guy named Sam Vedete told me. I had only met him at the tournament and had no idea of where he even went to school, but Sam and I eventually became close friends in college and then lifelong friends. This was just one example of how you could develop relationships with people in Utica who were outside your orbit.

Sports also meant getting "ink" for the first time. Your name was in print, you became known, and more people (especially older ones) recognized and interacted with you. UFA coaches appeared to check players out as well as to see the games. I knew who they were because my sister was a cheerleader at the Academy and because I had attended many of its football, basketball, and baseball home games even before she was there.

I marveled at the basketball team with players like Gary Evans and Wayne Decker, with Dick "Meatball" Rondenelli shooting his set shot from way out, and at Glen Stefano leading the football team. Bob Deep, as he was leaving football practice, often talked to us grade school kids when we were still playing fall baseball at a little make shift field in part of the formal Murnane Field areas. Those of us who played sports saw, spoke to and often met coaches and players on the high school and sometimes college level.

After one baseball game I pitched in 8th grade, Ed Swiecki, the UFA varsity football coach, came up and told me I'd be his quarterback one day. That I chose not to play football in high school would forever be a thorn in the side of my relationship with "Coach." But overall the transition from Hughes to UFA was made easier by the very strong continuity, between the two schools, of families, ball players, teachers, and coaches.

Eighth grade graduation was a dud to us odd-term students, since we left Hughes one day and entered high school almost the next. But I clearly remember not wanting to leave Hughes's warm cocoon. I was nervous. Every one of us who talked about it was.

1956 – The Nation

Ike beat Stevenson for the second time. His popularity may help to explain why the Democrats ran a previous loser. Ike was a sure winner no matter who the Democrats ran. He won basically every state except the Dixiecrat South, and the Electoral College by 457 to 73.

That fall, the world and the U.S. also faced two crises almost simultaneously. Egypt's dictator, Gamal Nasser, ordered his army to seize the Suez Canal, one of the world's most important waterways affecting the transportation of oil. The canal then under the control of the British, supported by France. The crisis was complicated by the Arab-Israeli war of that year. In Eastern Europe, the Polish people made a revolt against Soviet domination. A much more important revolt, complete with fierce fighting, broke out in Hungary. The Soviets moved in massive amounts of Russian troops to quell the revolt and restore the pro-Soviet puppet government.

Above all, Ike was a realist who understood both the pitfalls of military intervention and the war fatigue of the American people, who were also in the midst of an economic boom. He did not directly intervene in either arena, instead initiating settlement talks in the Middle East or tolerating Russian control of Eastern Europe. In both cases war was avoided, but some of our major allies, Israel, and the strongly anti-Soviet bloc in Congress disliked Eisenhower's response.

John Kennedy, a young senator from Massachusetts, made his national debut that year when he was nosed out for the Democratic vice presidential nomination by Estes Kefauver. Kefauver had made a name for himself through his Senate organized crime investigation and hearings. Losing the second spot in '56 was a blessing in disguise for JFK, since he couldn't be blamed at all for the ticket's dismal showing. Politics can turn losing into winning.

Films started to get a bit more controversial. Marilyn Monroe married the playwright Arthur Miller a scant two years after Joltin' Joe DiMaggio. No one knew who Arthur Miller was, and everyone felt bad for Joe. Eddie Fisher and Debbie Reynolds though, were Hollywood's good clean romance, adored by the nation. The shock of his throwing cute Debbie away for the actress whom even she concluded was "the most beautiful woman in the world" was yet to come. Clean Eddie was to become an Elizabeth Taylor's trophy husband. Hollywood scandal was a major social topic back then. Divorce, although less rare in Hollywood than in the country, had not been as public as it was in the Fisher-Reynolds-Taylor affair.

Music was something younger people found more and more important as rock and roll blossomed. Most songs of the day were about love, the perfect teenage topic. Although Elvis had burst onto the scene, here in Utica the Everly Brothers, Johnny Mathis, Buddy Holly, and Pat Boone were more popular.

Meanwhile, the technology of the Cold War was growing both impressively and dangerously. We invented the U-2 spy plane, and the Russians would soon shock the world with what they were developing in an effort to conquer space.

In Utica, Rufie Elefante, sensing continuing and growing problems with the press, had replaced Mayor Golder with John McKennan in the 1955 election. That change did not result in a letting-up of the corruption issues that had been raised since 1949 by the newspaper, but Elefante's control and ability to elect mayors remained unchallenged. When he was elected, Mayor McKennan even stated that he "owed it to one man." Voters did not appear to heed or care about the reported corruption. It was an early lesson in the adage that politically, "It's the economy, stupid." If money was being made, most people were employed with decent jobs, and personal and public spending were increasing, who cared about a bit of vice and corruption? People were generally happy with their lot in Utica life. The city government did provide excellent basic services.

About then was the only time I ever met Elefante. He had two favorite hangouts: his "Little City Hall" at Marino's restaurant in East Utica, and Uncle Henry's Pancake House downtown. My father, who was still a Rufie man, introduced me to the boss at Uncle Henry's. Elefante was nice, polite, and complimentary, but a man of few words on that occasion. When I tried to recall the meeting some years later, all I could think of was that he did not impress me as the "boss" type. Looks can be deceiving. No political leader, before or after, had the influence and control in Utica that Elefante engineered.

Utica Free Academy

UFA was the city's first public high school, the school where immigrant parents sent their children for a free American education. They viewed it as a great gift by a great country. When they attended UFA, my parents both walked there daily—one all the way from Jay to Kemble, the other a shorter walk from West Utica. Only when Proctor High was built did East Utica kids have the choice to attend a school closer to home.

I entered the halls of the Academy in the winter of 1957. The generation of my sister and me had little sense of what UFA meant to those we followed.

Freshman Year

The transition from a small neighborhood school to a very large city-wide one is unsettling, even when a student has a full summer to prepare. Odd-term students had no such luxury. In less than two weeks, we jumped from the cozy, easy-to-navigate Hughes to the tumultuous UFA. We went from seeing and interacting with no blacks to being integrated with many. We went from changing classrooms twice a day to changing every class, every hour. Instead of walking to school, we took either the early Sunset Avenue city bus or the more regularly running Genesee bus. If you missed the Sunset bus, you could run up to Genesee and catch a later one, or maybe get lucky by sticking your thumb out and hitching a ride. The bus rides did offer a glimpse of some very pretty girls riding to UFA and the two downtown Catholic high schools.

Finding classes the first week was quite difficult. Most of the older students laughed and misdirected freshmen; a few were helpful. Having a locker, in a locker room you shared with older students of mixed age, gender, and race, required memorizing a combination in order to deposit your coats, hats, and boots. A guy unknown to me, who I learned was named Dick Styc, had his locker close to mine. He was a body-builder type who had the reputation of being the strongest guy in school. He had a talent, which I was to see one day, of being able to rip the T-shirt he wore by a mere flex of his muscles! The first time I saw him do it, I was agape. By the way, he was a very nice guy.

My best Hughes friend, Dave Berkeley, and I both had a big advantage: guardian angels. Mike Slive lived across the street from "Berk" on Melrose. When we started at UFA, Mike—although not yet a senior—was already "all-everything." He was a star quarterback, top-level student, and president of his class. I knew him from the neighborhood, but not all that well. Since I hung with Berk, though, Mickey was extremely nice to me and a bit of his guardianship of Dave rubbed off on me. Berkeley was a character who had a good deal of moxie and, like me, was an athlete. At UFA he was to specialize in football.

His dad, who was still named Berkowitz, was a terrific guy who had a glass business but made his name with another venture. He started a new green stamps business to compete with the wildly successful nationwide S & H Green Stamp Co. The name is foreign now to people under 50, but was so popular in the '50s that Mr. Berkowitz thought he could make a good deal of money by copying and improving on its business model.

The model was pretty simple. You bought certain products and for every purchase you got some amount of green stamps. The more you bought and the more you spent, the more green stamps. You kept books of them and redeemed them for "free" products. It was like the "points reward" systems of today.

I do not recall Mr. B's program, but it offered better options than S & H. He introduced it locally and it took off. It didn't take S & H long to slap a huge lawsuit on him, resulting in a court injunction to shut him down. After quite a period of legal battles, Goliath slew David, or in this case my friend David's father. Today, Mr. Berkowitz would probably be a wealthy entrepreneur. David, both in being a nice guy and in having a good deal of his dad's moxie, is an example of the apple not falling far from the tree.

By the way, many readers even if they aren't from Utica might think they recognize the name Mike Slive. Mike went on to Dartmouth College, played football there, and then went to law school. He used his law and football backgrounds in a career with the NCAA, eventually becoming commissioner of the dominant South East Conference and nationally known. He retired as one of the most successful and well-known college sports administrators in America.

I was lucky, also, to have a couple of other angels guiding me during that first nervous year. Chet Patraitus and Walt Dziwis were upperclassmen, jocks, and friends of my older sister Bernie at UFA. (As a cheerleader, class of '56, she knew all the sports guys well.) Chet and Walt were also fellow Poles, in their case from West Utica. They took me under their wings, even to the point of sponsoring me for admission to their fraternity later that year.

On the first day I was especially nervous. My mother bought me a new red V-neck sweater, which I forgot to wear. Good thing I had a nice button-down shirt on. I rode the bus with some guys I knew. One, Dickie Barkett, was a star athlete from the Wankel Field area and Little League coach, Jack's son. I kind of hung with him and a few others as I entered the doors of the Academy.

The school was oddly segregated, in more ways than one. It seemed that boys knew to enter, and hang out in, the large stairway and lobby area on one side of the building, and the girls to take the other side. You didn't mix until the starting bell rang and everyone headed for their locker rooms. Black kids pretty much all hung together. Although the city's black population was tiny, at under 2 percent, all black kids of high school age attended UFA. The separation felt very strange, however. I had heard many stories about the black friends my sister had at school, and knew who most of the terrific athletes were. Everything I heard of the black sports figures was highly positive. When first entering the school, I had expected a different, more integrated kind of racial interaction.

Due to the size of the student population, lunchtime was split. The lunch room was huge and packed with kids. Those who didn't bring their lunch stood in the kitchen/cafeteria line across the hall and selected food to purchase. I quickly learned that the UFA mashed potatoes were the greatest. Whether I'd brought a sandwich or not, I always got at least one scoop.

I sat at a table of kids from my Hughes class, including my Hughes girlfriend. It took about two weeks for her to dump me for an older guy. The older guys swooped down on the good-looking freshman girls in a hurry.

Within a short time, my group at lunch and otherwise around school included guys that I'd played ball against in grade school and was now playing with at UFA. Several of us began playing freshman basketball right away. Players including Joe Prymas and Bob Gilberti from Kernan School, Harold Hanson from Roosevelt, and others hung together. My Hughes buddies Jeff, Jake, and Berk continued to be among my teammates and friends. It was clear from the outset that at UFA, jocks kept in tight knit groups.

The UFA Faculty

Looking back, later in life, on my high school educational experience and how directed and challenging it was the first year, I better understood the value of UFA. Ms. Maderer, Roger D'Aprix, "Mag," and Hazel Cutter were as good as they come at that level.

The two Maderer sisters, I think twins, taught at UFA. Freshman Algebra was expertly instructed by "Sexy Maderer," the sister built very well and gawked at by the boy students. We did not mind when she came close as she checked our homework. Flirt we did.

Miss Maggiolino, "Mag," was perhaps the best teacher I had in high school. She had a canny ability to know when you were ill-prepared to translate the day's Latin assignment. And if you stumbled, she mercilessly took you apart in front of the class. You quickly learned to learn your Latin. She was the proverbial little spitfire with a heart of gold underneath all the toughness. It was assumed that she was seeing the very affected English teacher, Mr. Eddington—or "Duke," as he was called by students who thought playing on the name of Duke Ellington was clever. They eventually married.

Roger D'Aprix was an English teacher in a class all by himself. I think he eventually taught at prep schools. With him and Miss. Hand I finally started to read seriously; I recall, for example, how Hemingway captured my interest and imagination.

Cutter, Hymes, Parritano and Betty Pritchard, my wonderful homeroom teacher, all taught history classes. The stimulating discussions they encouraged were more college style than high school. One, however, predicted in 1959 that Castro would not last a year! She did make the claim that "we" would boot him out. I guess she foresaw the Bay of Pigs with a better result than turned out.

I can't remember my freshman science courses or teachers. I spent four years in high school, four in college, and one in graduate school with no interest in that subject matter. My grades showed it.

It is often said that the freshman year in high and college is the most difficult. I did not find that to be true. Study was not all that hard, the teachers were excellent, and in basketball I was immediately successful.

Jeff Jacobson and I quickly moved into key starting roles on the freshman team under the coaching of Ed Swiecki. Oddly, he played me, probably because of my 6'2" height, on the inside, with my back to the basket on offense. This was strange, considering that my forte at Hughes was outside shooting and passing. Oh well, the team and both Jake and I were successful nevertheless. I recall just two coaching expressions of Swiecki; "When in doubt, dribble out" and "He who hesitates is lost." He was obviously more of a football coach. But he was fierce about winning and pushing us to play hard. He gave no quarter to players who dogged it or made mistakes. I continue, at age 74, to hear him yelling at me, "Potocki, you bonehead!"

High school coaching in my era was limited. Most coaches were not technically trained and lacked great experience in the sports they coached. We were not taught the mechanics of our sports, or subjected to customized training. We were forbidden to weightlift, for fear we might become muscle-bound. I don't think even many of the football players lifted. And no one went to specialized sports camps, if they existed at all.

We did not even learn what a "screen" in basketball was. When I played in an older-guy league on a terrific Marcy State team between high school and college, players like Mike Damsky, Nonnie Pensero, Pete Pentasuglia , Dick Miller, John Brigantino, Joe Wolonowski and Bull Fabio showed how the game could be so much easier by setting screens, switching men on defense seamlessly or boxing out for rebounding. Mike, with his huge size, set the best screens of anyone I ever played with on any level. In high school baseball, no coach taught me about pitch count, changing speeds, or how to hold the ball for different pitches. We just went out and threw hard.

I grew to realize, though, that certain coaches for several key reasons made us want to win for them. It was chemistry and emotion, not skill instruction that provided us an invaluable weapon and learning skill for all aspects of life. Fred Collins, who coached both varsity basketball and baseball, was the epitome of a coach who moved you emotionally to want to win. Swiecki did that too for many of his football players. I also had a great opportunity to play with older players, which elevates both your "game" and your aspiration to excel. Many played at UFA.

I knew Jerry Coon from the Parkside ball field days and Tony Redmond from the Hughes connection with his mother who taught there. To butt heads in pick-up games with Eldred "Corncob" Johnson, Ted Martin, and Joe Rivers was quite an experience of awe and respect. They were the top black players in the school. As I immediately noticed, the question of race never came up among the players. Sports are great equalizers on the court, field, and track. And one black player I knew nothing about at the time, and hadn't played against, immediately struck me as special.

I first noticed him at a varsity game I attended after that afternoon's freshman game. His name was Ed Hill. He made a move to the basket that made my jaw drop. We would quickly get to know each other.

The racial divide was clear in the classroom, but only as I look back on the times. Virtually all of my Hughes friends and I, like most whites, were known as "college-prep" students; our courses were designed to allow us to meet college admissions standards. I do not recall having one black student in any of my classes. Blacks were basically in "shop" classes if male and secretarial ones if female. The segregation was not fully grasped by us white students, but was purposefully engineered by school counselors. I did not fully understand the bitterness of feeling about this segregation until I was an adult and discussed it with friends like Ed Hill. What became obvious to me as I reached the end of high school was that many good black athletes who were prized by colleges could not be recruited because of their lack of college-prep coursework. Players like Ed were cheated by the system—a problem that will be discussed later in the book.

I marvel at today's high-school dropout rate among African American males, which is at a scandalous level for an age of "diversity" at any cost in most colleges, sensitivity to racial issues on the part of high schools, and great professional opportunities. In contrast, every single black friend I had in my four years at UFA graduated, even with the educational deck stacked against them. Unlike black students' options today, their options were limited, yet they stuck it out and stayed in school.

Social Life Takes Hold

The lay of the social and extracurricular land became clear over the next few months as I grew from a shy, somewhat intimidated freshman to one who grew friendships and learned his way around.

There were two social hot spots that served as after-school places where you went if you wanted to be popular with the "in" crowd. The first was the Square View Dinette on Oneida Square, a couple of blocks from both UFA and St. Francis. It was the more "preppy" place to go for a soda after school, to flirt with girls and have some harmless fun with the guys.

Although most of the guys who hung out there were from UFA, many of the girls were from St. Francis. That resulted in an interesting dynamic: UFA guys meeting and eventually dating St. Francis girls. I would be one of them.

The Square View crowd pretty much drank cokes, ate French fries, smoked, and played the jukebox. When we sipped a coke for a couple of hours, it drove the owner a bit nuts since he was not making much money. He constantly harassed the students, who pretty much paid no attention to him, while his son, who worked there, tried to hold everything together. The atmosphere, the activities, and the clientele were very different at another hang out but a few doors away on the Square.

Masters' was the gathering place for shooting pool and gambling on pinball machines. The waiting lines were long, particularly for the pinball. Without getting too much into the weeds of gambling, it worked like this in pinball: You got points for reaching certain levels before losing your balls. Then, after you achieved a certain number of points, you were paid money by the management. The more points, the more money; the better you were, the more points you compiled. You quickly learned that the games at Masters' were difficult to master (pun intended). As teenagers, not many of us realized that the "house" never loses in the long run.

The most popular pool game was "pill pool." A bunch of numbered little balls, or "pills," were shaken and each player got one at random. Whoever got his ball into the pocket first won the pot of money. The pot's value was determined at the start of the game on a per-man basis. If four players played for a dollar per game, the pot would be $4, the winner taking a net of $3. Some played for high stakes, others for low ones. The "house" didn't care, since the shooters rented the table for a set time. So, skill did matter.

I wasn't much good at pool or pinball, but like most boys, gave into temptation anyway. I learned not to play the hard way—by losing money.

The source of my modest income was still my paper route. The evenings I collected customer payments, along with the cash I had collected from selling papers at the hospital, ended with a trip on the bus to Masters' usually to play pinball. I quickly realized I could not afford these trips. I lost money as most players did. I had also bagged the paper route given the school time dynamics of study and sports. Cash flow was tight. One of my last nights at Masters' was the most exciting, and had nothing to do with what went on there.

Wayne Delwo and Mike Detraglia, UFA football players I then knew only from afar, came in—Mike bloodied. They were part of a group of UFA guys, mainly other football players, who had gone to Proctor Park in East Utica for a previously agreed-upon fight with some Proctor High guys. Mike was a spitting image of what Nicholas Cage would look like in "Peggy Sue Got Married," only better-looking although not that night. Wayne was a big guy whose good looks could fool you about his ability to fight. Both were tough guys.

They and the few others were ambushed by a much larger group armed with chains, bats, and a few knives. Our guys had no chance and were badly whipped. Masters 'was alive with excitement. As an observer, so was I. It was all like something out of a teenage rumble movie, complete with a sympathetic stars.

The Master's atmosphere—a tough crowd, gambling and shooting pool while listening to Buddy Holly's "That'll Be the Day"—was on the edge. The touch of sin was a kind of excitement you didn't find at the Square View.

Another iconic hangout every Friday night, particularly during basket-ball season, was Garramone's Restaurant on Eagle Street. Everybody went there for pizza—UFA, St. Francis, and Utica Catholic Academy kids. Every square inch of every booth and table was packed. John, the owner, seemed torn between selling a lot of pizza and wishing all the teens would go away. One could not blame him, the noise alone was deafening.

The top social events for high school kids were the dances at St. Francis, on Fridays during the no-basketball seasons, and weekly dances held at the city's Parkway skating rink in the summertime.

I started to attend the St. Francis dances in the spring of my freshman year after I became a member of the Phi Delta fraternity. When I met fraternity brother, Brian Bigelow, who was a year and a half ahead of me in school, we immediately hit it off. Brian would become the clos-est friend I had in high school and beyond; indeed, he was the closest I came to having a brother.

Bris and I along with Mike O'Hare, and other Phi Delt guys attended the dances, as did many ball-player friends like Joe Prymas and Bob

Gilberti. Guys would cluster in "guy" groups, girls in "girl" groups. As the records of "Come Go with Me," "Whole Lotta Shakin'Goin' On," "Bye Bye Love," and Johnny Mathis love songs played, some guys would split and ask a girl to dance. All the while, Father O'Neil patrolled to keep order. I do not remember one incident of fighting or even arguing at the dances. Every dance offered a fun, good time.

At one of the dances, I was smitten by a New Hartford High girl. It was rare for any New Hartford student to attend a dance or school gathering in Utica. And we sure didn't go to theirs. The girl, Sharon Davies, was in a sorority to which many St. Francis girls belonged. I think it was Sub Deb.

I mention my first high-school flirtation for a couple of reasons. Sharon was a couple of years older. Realizing that immediately, I upped my age and grade by a year. (It stuck, since I was with mostly older guys.) That spring she asked me to her junior prom. We doubled with her friend, whose date drove. We went to a bar in Frankfort that served minors without hesitation and played decent dance music. Like many high school kids at the time in the area, Sharon smoked, and she put the first cigarette I ever had in my mouth. So here I was: a high school freshman, with an older girl, drinking and smoking. Like Bill Clinton with weed, I didn't inhale, at first.

As most kids my age in the '50s, I was in a hurry to grow up. And boys were given great latitude, by parents and by society in general. The very thought of hanging around the house, doing stuff with parents or depending on parents, was not a common desire among '50s teens. We wanted to be "out" as soon as possible.

Sharon was good-looking, nice, and easygoing. As my birthday on May 31 approached, I realized that my age lie would be exposed, since she expected me to drive. Embarrassed, I simply never called her, and I don't think I ever saw her again.

I continued to be an occasional smoker. Nearly everyone smoked, including most ball players at UFA. It was not banned, and coaches never even raised smoking and drinking as issues. My goodness, Whitey Ford did cigarette ads on TV, and both managers and players smoked in dugouts. Mickey Mantle, Hank Bauer, and Billy Martin were dubbed the Copacabana Kids by New York newspapers because of their carousing.

New Hartford High did require that all athletes sign a pledge not to drink or smoke while on a team. The penalty was expulsion from the sport. Looking back, I wish UFA had done the same for both health and conditioning reasons. But the dangers to both were not yet fully grasped. At the time, many of us believed our New Hartford counterparts were not having as much fun as we were.

Our fraternity, Phi Delta, held a house party once in a while at our president's parents' house. He, Jim Lee, was the son of a local doctor. Their house featured a large finished basement, complete with a bar. The perfect party setting it was.

At one party, I was sitting on a couch next to a girl who was all over me. I was baffled at how she was trying to kiss. I had no idea of what a French kiss was! Sex was not yet a topic for many at my age. Even movie kissing was lips-only. Husband and wife slept apart in single beds. Sex was only implied in movies—and, by the way, much sexier. To take the male viewer's breath away, Marilyn Monroe didn't have to do anything but appear. After all, even Joe D succumbed to her charm and style. We considered parties such as this one adult-like and fun. The high school frat party was yet another example of our rush to grow up.

UFA Baseball, the Beginning

April marked the start of high school baseball. For reasons I didn't understand but did not question, my father urged me to try out for the varsity team. It was unheard-of in those days for a freshman to make a varsity team and play. Feeling out of place, I plunged in and showed up for tryouts.

The positions I played were pitcher and first base, the same ones I had played all along. I threw well and was the only backup player for the starting first baseman, who was Ted Martin, the basketball star. Ted treated me so well that I never forgot it.

Our home ball field was Murnane, which most of us walked to from school for the tryouts. The field was a good hike from school. I was one of several players who walked there with Ted. He was highly instructive to this young kid, encouraging me and giving me tips on both playing first base and hitting. As I learned many years later of his very skillful business successes, I was not surprised. He sure knew how to treat people well and to motivate.

I made the team and worked out daily. When it was my turn to take infield practice, I was terrorized by the velocity of the first-base throw by our third baseman, Fred Gachowski. He threw a rising bullet that I feared was going to hit me right in the face. I had the same fear every time he threw over, but somehow I toughed it out. Martin would stand behind me on the side and laugh. It was part of a young kid's welcome to high-level high school sports.

My guess is that Ted did not realize the impression he made on a freshman white kid. Admiring this star black player was completely natural for me, with not a thought of race. Sports at UFA was a great equalizer at a time when blacks were still being lynched in the South, where Ted and I could not even have been on the same team! The race question was more complicated and perplexing in Utica as a whole, but at UFA, at least within the sports community, relations were positive and harmonious. The issue went much deeper than I could ever realize in 1957. I would sense it more by the end of the decade, but did not get close to grasping it until I was much older. Ed Hill and Cecil Brandon, who would be basketball, and in Hill's case also baseball, teammates of mine over the next few years, would play an important role in my fully understanding race relations in Utica in that period and how they shaped lives.

The '57 team experience was the start, in a serious way, of my high school athletic journey, a journey that ultimately had its highs and lows, negatives and positives. High school sports puffs kids' egos, provides lifelong memories and relationships, breaks some hearts, and teaches how to handle the ups and downs that occur throughout life.

That '57 baseball team was excellent. It featured Dick Barkett, a top-notch center fielder; Roger Bennett, a very good pitcher; Larry Tozzi , a great pitcher; Jerry Murawski and Stan Kuklinski , both infielders; my old neighborhood friend Steve Jacobson, and my former Little League, teammate Les Lewis, one of the best "dead fastball" hitters around. I was proud that I was to be part of such a good team. It didn't dawn on me that I would sit on the bench all season and be miserable. But that was not to be. I was to be part of the pitching staff on the 58 team that featured many of the same players.

As we were warming up for the opening game, I noticed as I stood next to Ted, waiting to step in for my turn to take throws, a school bus pull into the parking lot. It was not the other team, since they were already there.

Out jumped Coach Swiecki , who was coaching the junior varsity team. He walked right over to me, took me by the arm, and said: "Potocki, you're pitching for me today." I got on the bus and opened the JV season on the mound. I have no idea, nor did I ever ask if varsity Coach Collins knew, what was going on. He never said a word to me.

It all worked out for the best since I got a lot of action, the team was the best JV team around, and we had a great bunch of guys. The pitcher who had beaten us in grade school, Leo Latore, also pitched, as did Jim Ward. Jerry Lysik was an excellent all-around athlete and a good hitter. Jerry Briggs, Tom Price, and Joey Prymas, just to mention a few, excelled. Ed Hill was our third baseman and sparked the entire team, game after game. Latore moved away at the end of the year, but many on that team later formed a championship team, in 1959.

The first half of my freshman year could not have been better. Very good grades, successful sports, and fun including having a first high school girlfriend albeit briefly. Then came summer.

Work, Ball, and No Dates

Summer vacation hadn't started yet when my father announced, one evening, that he had found me a job. At 14, I was to have my first real summer job. That was not unusual. Every guy I knew of my age and older had a summer job. You got your government working papers at 14 and you went to work, to make some money. The parents of my middle-class buddies didn't have the money to send their kids to special camps or take them on trips. The need to work, and the expectation that you would, were taken for granted.

The job was mowing the lawn around the graves at Calvary Cemetery on upper Oneida Street. The walk to work from Cornwall Ave. was short. I was both excited and afraid, while determined to tough it out no matter what.

The gentleman—and I do mean gentleman, in the broadest sense of the word—who ran the operation was Mr. Deck, who my father knew from the old days. I was sort of eager to work there, because one of the older employees was Bill Deck, one of the best athletes in the Utica area. I had frequently watched him play baseball at Murnane Field for the always-dominant Marcy State Hospital team in the Utica

MUNY League. The league was top-notch, featuring many great players spanning a wide age range. (More about it later.) The Marcy State Hospital team—with players like Bill Deck, Dick Miller, Alan Gilberti, Howie Kane, Roger Lemke, and "Chops" Bohanna was the crème de la crème of the league.

I was a bit star-struck to be working side by side with Billy Deck. I also figured that he knew of my being a future UFA star and would take me under his wing on the job. Nothing like what I imagined happened. Deck and the other big guys working at the cemetery barely noticed or paid attention to me. And I was scared to death to approach them. I hung with the other grass-cutter, who was slightly older than I and much friendlier.

My mother made my daily brown-bagged lunch. The first day on the job, I put it on a shelf in the room where we all ate lunch. When I returned to eat it, it was gone; someone had stolen it. I did not have the guts, at all, to go over to the older guys and demand my lunch. I also had the good sense not to complain to Mr. Deck. Thank God I had a little money in my pocket, so I could run across the street to the Ridgewood Market and buy a pack of cupcakes and a soda. That was my lunch for a week. Every day, my mother's nice lunch was taken and I had the cupcakes. That was my initiation fee, and Bill Deck didn't lift a finger to stop it. I think Don Deck also worked there. I've known Don over the years, but have never asked him who the lunch thief was. I'm sure they all had a hand in it (or, better said, bites of it). And at that point, Bill Deck most likely had no idea who I was.

These older guys did all of the heavy work, such as digging the graves, for which they got the big bucks. So we cutters, worked the mowers alone. That did allow us to take some liberties, such as leaving the mowers running way up on the hill and taking naps behind gravestones.

I had a part-time job as well. My friend Brian Bigelow worked as a stock clerk at a little store on Oswego Street called Nugent's. The wonderful Mr. and Mrs. Nugent owned and operated it. Brian lived around the corner from the store, on Waverly Place.

Somehow, I don't recall how, "Big" earned enough to take a 2- or 3-week trip to Europe. He asked me, and I agreed, to work at Nugent's stocking shelves a couple of nights a week while he was away. Upon meeting me, the owners, after meeting me, agreed.

Taking the city bus back and forth, I worked in the extremely small, and very hot, stock room upstairs gathering items for the store's shelves as needed. I soon discovered the warm—actually hot—beer upstairs and occasionally treated myself to a bottle. I then hid the empty and dumped it outside as I left. I'm sure the Nugent's realized what I was up to, but they didn't say a word.

I was not quite sure what it was, but I felt great riding the bus to and from the store. Looking back on it, I'm sure it was due to my feeling older. Most boys my age rushed to act independently, as I've said, and that of course included making money. That will sound strange to a 14-year-old today.

One memory of those Nugent days sticks with me: getting on the Genesee bus to go home and hearing "Wake up Little Suzy" blaring on a car radio as the bus door opened. I stepped on that bus feeling very good about life. It's odd that a particular summer, or summers, in a young person's life inspire what was at the time a profound feeling, which stays within the memory, not to be forgotten. As I write, I see myself stepping on that bus in the summer of '57.

Baseball and the '57 Yankees

That summer, I made the decision to forsake the South Utica Babe Ruth League, which was for players age 13 to 15, for the Utica PONY

League, whose players were 14 and 15. The choice was easy, since I wanted to play with my UFA buddies, many of whom were my JV teammates. A good number of local public high school players played in the PONY League, while the Catholic school players, mainly from South Utica, stuck with Babe Ruth. My decision was another break of my South Utica athletic ties.

I played for Tri- State Laundry, the West Utica team. Our coach Tom Price was the son of Jack Price, the longtime league president. Tom Jr. ("Tick") and I played together at UFA. I can't recall whether it was Tri -State or our league All Star team that was invited to Yankee Stadium attend game, which included a visit to the Yankee locker room. II was a once-in-a-lifetime thrill.

This was "the" Yankees, the perennial world champions except for the rare Dodgers blip of '55. They were the Yankees of Mantle, Berra, Ford, Kubic, Richardson, Larsen, Skowron, Billy Martin, Elston Howard and others. A teammate and I spoke with Jerry Coleman, the team's sec- ond baseman. The Utica Daily Press even published a picture of the three of us, along with an article about the trip. I'm sure the top notch Yankee publicity arm sent the article to the local outlet.

As Coleman was talking with us, he looked at me and asked if I want- ed to play in the majors someday. I said "Sure, Mr. Coleman." He said: "Well, if you do grow good enough to make the majors, there is only one team to play for. Do you want to know which team that is?" Playing along with him, I answered: "Sure." He replied: "It's the Yankees, do you want to know why?" "Sure, Mr. Coleman." He looked at me all serious, squarely in the eye, and explained: "Because we've got all the money!" How about that for an honest answer to a young guy? Money became a Yankee hating reason as they were too often be accessed of buying pennants while other teams were on shaky financial footings.

I didn't understand the full breath of Coleman's remark to me until many years later as I read David Halberstam's wonderful, "Summer of '49." The book describes, the young, newly married Yankee rookie who could barely afford to eat as he vied for a roster spot in spring training. Not until he made the team and became a regular did he achieve financial stability and probably always blessed the Yankees for it. He was passing the message of solid, you can count on, Yankee money onto a young kid from Utica. By the way, Coleman's rookie year salary was $5,000!

Historically though, Utica was Yankee country. In the days before free agency, major leaguers earned extra money by barnstorming around towns during off season and playing against local teams. They occasionally played exhibitions in Utica. Yankee players embraced some local spots including their favorite restaurant, Ventura's in east Utica. To this day, autographed pictures of great Yankee players hang on the restaurant's walls. In the late 1960's the incomparable Joe DiMaggio played in a gin rummy game on the second floor with Rufie Ventura and the then mayor of Utica, Dick Assaro. There has been little Yankee hating in Utica.

Rejection

The summer of '57 brought no success chasing girls, although not much effort went into that sport. A staple entertainment in the summer was the outdoor city-funded dances at the Parkway skating rink, where the youth and senior center is today. A large number of kids from various high schools attended, but it was mostly UFA kids with a good dose of Proctor types, especially guys looking for trouble.

The somewhat violent rivalry between the UFA and Proctor football players, as seen in the Mike Detraglia-Master's story I have recounted, spilled over into the summer and occasionally broke out at the dances.

At one, the first I attended that summer, a group of Proctor guys and ex-Proctor types attacked UFA's great defensive end, Chuck Kokhanowski. Chuck was some tough guy. Along with the likes of Andy Putrello, Pat Korie, Bob Saptuzzi, and Ray Stefano, he made life miserable for high school offenses. He regularly raided backfields, knocking opposing quarterbacks on their behinds.

The scene at the dance was: Paul Anka blaring out "Diana" as Chuck ran around the big circle, stopping here and stopping there to punch out the guys chasing him. Run, stop; pop-pop; run, stop; pop-pop, as the music took on a pulsating beat while all the girls started screaming. The line plea to Diana to stay seemed to last forever. In real time it was a brief fight, halted by off-duty cops working as security men. But what a rush it was to see Chuck take on the entire bunch.

At the same dance, I spotted the two girls I thought were the best-looking at UFA, Sue Krupski and Linda Lasher. They stood with a group of older guys who looked like a mix of UFA and Proctor types, definitely seniors or even recent graduates. The two girls were class of '60 and not much older than I, but as I had already learned, good-looking young girls attracted the older guys.

I tried to hide my gawking, and walked as close as I could to them, as my friends and I circled the dance floor. Linda was also a wickedly good jitterbug dancer. I was much too shy and unsure of myself to ask her to dance. One of my friends offered to approach her on my behalf. He did, asking if she'd dance with me. Looking on from some yards away, I noticed a smile as she glanced toward me. My hopes were up. My friend returned and informed me that she had very nicely and politely said: "No, thank you." I turned red and walked away.

We danced a lot a few years later, though, when we dated for a spell. Linda was a very nice person, a good friend and a fun date. She came from a family that I was lucky to get to know a bit. And she still did a wicked jitterbug. Linda married a baseball pitcher of great talent, Dick Raymer, without a doubt the best thrower in the history of Utica Catholic Academy.

Fall of '57

I upset Coach Swiecki big-time, even before the semester started, due to my not trying out for the freshman football team. His idea that I would be his future quarterback was not to be. My parents thought playing football was a terrible idea, since my main sports interests and talents were in basketball and baseball. Why risk an injury that could bring those sports to an end? I agreed. I knew little to nothing about football and was not a "hit 'em" kind of guy. In fact, I was a bit of a softie. And, wouldn't you guess, in September I did something really dumb.

I agreed to play in a pickup football game between a St. Francis team and my fraternity. My mother went, as kids often said in those days, ape shit. After a huge argument, she said I could play if I wore a helmet and shoulder pads. I agreed, and she went out and bought them.

Game day was cold. Although it wasn't raining, it had rained the day and evening before, making the ground wet. I was the only one who showed up with equipment. The St. Francis crew, most of whom I knew from South Utica, protested and said I could not play with it. My friend and frat brother Stew Pratt begged me to walk away. I did not, and played—as running back, no less.

As sure as, in the words of Groucho Marx, "Grant took Richmond" (wrong Marx quote—and Grant never did), I got hurt. In the latter part of the game, I carried the ball, got a big yardage gain, was tackled and wound up on my back. Before I could jump up, a big fat kid from the other team came crashing on top of me, knees first. Everyone heard the loud snap of something breaking. The game immediately stopped.

Luckily we were playing at Murnane, directly across from Faxton hospital. Since the cell phone and 911 were many decades away, a couple of guys ran over to the hospital to ask for help. It came well over an hour later. I was carried off the field, wet and freezing, to the hospital.

My parents arrived quickly. My mother was hysterical and angry. The injury was a broken collarbone. I'd also caught a mild case of pneumonia while lying on the wet ground. I was admitted to the hospital for two or three days. My only question to Dr. Friedman was: "Will I be able to play basketball this season?" Basketball season was around the corner, with varsity tryouts soon to start.

I exited the hospital a few days later and returned to school in a shoulder harness. Of course, many kids patted me on the shoulder in greeting. Why do I tell this story? Two reasons.

Teenagers think they are indestructible, and always think they know more than their parents. That is a characteristic that transcends generations, often bringing harm to both parents and teens. As it turned out, my injury was not due to football. It was an act of cruelty and stupidity.

A person I know today, who attended St. Francis at the time of the game, told me not long ago that I was a target going into the game. Evidently the halls of the school were full of chatter about my injury, which was considered, mission accomplished.

That confirms the feeling I had as a young man that there was a tension among South Utica Catholics about my being "off the reservation." As an adult, I became friends with few of the guys from Friar Tech, the St. Francis nickname, who'd either played in that game or knew of it. Even as adults, they still carried an anti-black bias. How much did my playing ball with blacks have to do with the resentment that urged and encouraged my injury that day? Or was I just disliked for "leaving the South Utica fold?"

I cannot conclude my recollections of UFA football without mentioning the '57 team, many of whom were Class of '58 graduates. In addition to the defensive players mentioned earlier, Mike Slive, Larry Tozzi, Dick Barkett, Les Lewis, Ed Hill, Jerry Lysic, Morris Allen, Bob Marx, Chet Patraitus and others formed one of the best teams in the long history of UFA and of the city. They won the Central Oneida and City League titles in high style including defeating a very good Proctor team.

All high school classes experience premature tragedy, tough loss, and sadness. The UFA class of this talented and tenacious football team was no exception.

Chuck Kokhanowski—the indestructible defensive end—died as a young man while serving our country in Germany. Chuck was killed in a car crash.

Several years ago, I read that Chet Patraitus—nice, fun-loving Chet—had passed away. Even though he no longer lived here and I had not seen him since high school, I went to his funeral at Holy Trinity Church out of thanks and respect for the brief friendship we did have. The West Utica kid returned to the mecca of West Utica Catholicism for his send-off to heaven. The only one of the old UFA bunch I saw there was Andy Putrello. We greeted each other and spoke upon leaving the church. We fondly remembered Chet, and UFA, and others who had passed on. Andy, a wonderful man, was active for years in local boxing, both as a boxer himself and helping young kids learn the sport. He became a master craftsman in bricklaying and concrete, much like the Italian masters, while building a successful contracting company. Andy was a solid kid at UFA, who is even more solid as a man.

'57-'58, School and Basketball

That fall semester, the second half of my freshman year, was much like the first, with the same teachers and the same good grades. As the year progressed, I became less interested in study and more interested in sports and social life. Coasting in the classroom was becoming a habit. Having fun proved more enticing than hitting the books.

As the basketball tryouts approached, I was not able to participate because of my football injury. I assumed I would wind up on the JV team. I was shocked when the Varsity team names were posted at the gym and I was on the list. My Hughes and freshman teammate and friend Jeff Jacobson made the team as well.

I felt very odd and more than a bit embarrassed. I was convinced there were other players who had earned their way on during tryouts while I didn't. Not far in the back of my mind was an awareness that a couple of black players who weren't listed on the team's roster were good enough to make the grade. I realized later, however, that Coach Collins knew what he was doing. He had a certain vision of his future team, and I was being groomed to be part of it.

Even though our team was not very good that year, I as a second-term freshman and first-term sophomore sat the bench. Practices were great, but I couldn't stand not playing in games. Another player, Claude Vance, felt the same way. We asked Collins midway through the season to send us down to the JV team. He did, and we both started played a lot of court minutes.

On the JV team, I returned to my zone of comfort on the outside, playing the forward position and exhibiting a very good, long- range shot. In those days, there was no three-point line. My range was way beyond that of today's high school three-pointer. The other forward on the team, Cecil Brandon, had a similar range and shot. Very good. The JV move was a good one since it gave me comfort, confidence, and a reputation as a shooter-scorer.

The '57-'58 varsity team was a bust, winning only seven games. But Collins was not discouraged. He was quoted at the end of the season saying: "We are going to be a powerhouse next year." The team he had been carefully cultivating in his mind would become real in '58-'59.

'57-'58: The Nation Meets Utica

Two national events of that period actually had significant local implications.

In October of 1957, the Russians launched the first man-made satellite into space, Sputnik. It's interesting that the name translates in English to "fellow traveler." The shock of being beaten by the Russians in the fields of science and technology was a blow to our country's collective ego. We were supposed to be first in everything! A shocked nation did not understand how a communist country of limited means could be more advanced in missile technology than a country with the best standard of living on the planet.

Many blamed Ike, and the issue quickly became political. Why Ike? He was a budget skinflint and wasn't spending a lot of taxpayers' money on missile technology or space exploration. He believed in tight budgets and limited taxation. That formula was bringing America prosperity and enviable job growth.

Sputnik opened up a barrage of Democratic criticism, which ultimately led to the "missile gap" issue John F. Kennedy used against Richard Nixon, Ike's vice president, in the 1960 election. That issue assisted the paper-thin Kennedy win. It's ironic that JFK later had to face a near-nuclear war over Russian missiles placed in Cuba.

Sputnik also caused a rush in Congress to catch up to Russia, which translated into more money spent on defense, missile development, and space exploration programs. This money gave a big boost to giant defense companies like GE and Bendix. Some of it found its way to Utica, creating more jobs and adding to the boost those companies gave the local economy. Sputnik was, therefore, a blessing in disguise for Utica.

One event highlighting the importance of the major defense company in Utica, General Electric, was the appearance of Ronald Reagan who visited in the late 50's. Reagan, then a spokesman for the company and the host of a GE- sponsored TV show, gave a talk on national defense and technology that played into the Cold War, anti-Russian theme. It is no accident that he ultimately became President of the United States as a Cold War warrior who, with others such as Margaret Thatcher and Pope John Paul II, led the effort to bring down the Soviet Union.

The second national event, this one shaking the city with a profoundly negative impact, involved the criminal underworld.

In November, a state trooper stumbled onto a meeting held in the sleepy village of Apalachin in New York's southern tier. The "Apalachin Convention" became instant national news.

It was a meeting of about 100 Mafiosi from all over the U.S., held to discuss some internal problems and how power would be divvied up. As was mentioned in the book's opening, three attendees were from Utica. This meeting would ultimately lead to important change in the political landscape of Utica, and in the city's statewide and national image.

Since the late '40s, the Utica newspaper had been campaigning against political corruption. Its target was the Democratic political boss and leader, Rufus Elefante. But that campaign had gained little traction in the city, particularly as it impacted local elections.

Now, in 1957, a major Mafia influence in Utica was exposed as fact. That caused an outcry which finally found its way to Albany, the seat of state government. Utica instantly became an embarrassment that could no longer be swept under the rug and ignored.

Gubernatorial and legislative action which, a year or so later, led to the launching of the Fischer Investigation that would bring sweeping change to the city.

Change Rushes In

By the beginning of '58, the core of my high school friendships formed as my grades started to tumble. The formula by which good friends and having a good time contribute to lower grades is time-tested.

Brian Bigelow, Bob Gilberti, Phil Obernesser and I became an inseparable foursome. Brian and Phil were older and members of the class of '59 while Bob, better known as "Owl," and I were both odd-termers of the Class of '61. How and why we meshed as a group is still a bit perplexing to me.

"Big" has already been described a little, but it is worth repeating that you would be hard-pressed to find a better friend: pleasant, good-looking, friendly, always smiling. Everyone who knew him embraced him. He was your typical Mr. Popular high school student, of the "gentleman's B and C" type in the classroom with an A+ in social standing. He was not athletic, but had great charm. He was the only high school friend I had who did not play a sport. That he was actually my best friend broke the mold even more.

The odd thing about Brian was the black cloud that seemed to follow him. For reasons hard to grasp to this day, he frequently became the target of guys who did not know him. For example, I recall one UFA dance when a boy walked up to him and slapped him on the head. Not a word was said that could have prompted this, and the fact that we "pretty big men on campus" types were standing right alongside of our friend did not deter the assault. Brian had no idea who the kid was. In addition, Brian was accident-prone. On the one hand, he glowed, but on the other, he had that small bit of bad luck and worry that seemed to darken or threaten his glow. I feel his glow to this day.

The "Owl," Gilberti, was a legend in his own time. The best way to describe him was that he was a funnier, more cutting, cleverer, brasher Don Rickles than Don Rickles. He was a big, strong football player, who had an owl-like facial expression and kept night-owl hours from an early age on. He cut up everyone, and they loved it. His heart of gold was easily recognized. To be insulted by the Owl was to have made it. He never studied, always bluffed his way through the classroom, drank beer starting at age 14, smoked, and was enjoyed, amused, and liked by all who knew him. He gave everyone nicknames including mine, "Stick," for tall and skinny. The nicknames he gave girls, even the ones he dated, should not be repeated here. One Owl story sort of sums him up.

Occasionally in the summertime, our group would take a Sunday afternoon trip to a bar named Di Castro's at Sylvan Beach. It was a hot dance spot with live band music. We once went when both Owl and I were still too young to drive, let alone order a drink. All of us were "carded" at the door. In our circle and beyond, most of us under the 18- year-old drinking age carried fake ID of some sort in case we were carded, an expression stemming from the draft card all males at 18 received from Uncle Sam. Owl carried his brother Cy's former military ID. Cy was considerably older than the Owl—by well over a dozen years. The guy checking IDs at the entrance took one look at the card and at Owl, knowing instantly that the youth in front of him couldn't possibly be as old as the card said. He was all set to keep him out when the Owl looked at him and bellowed, "Whaddya mean, I drove Ike to the Geneva Convention." All of us, including the door guy, burst out laughing. He was laughing so hard that he waved us all in.

Phil certainly wasn't Owl-like. I knew him a bit from the South Utica Little League days, and he also played on our '57 JV baseball team. "Obie" had transferred from St. Francis to UFA. He was a rebel and could not take the rigidity the Catholic Brothers imposed on the male

St. Francis students. There, boys and girls were separated and guys who stepped out of line were smacked around by the Brothers. A dress code was also in place. It was no surprise to anyone who knew him that Phil was not long for St. Francis.

Phil was extremely bright, a crew-cut Ivy-looking type, sometimes too blunt, and moody. He also was very clever with quips that usually sailed above most of our heads. It did not take long in Obie's company to realize that not far beneath the surface, he had a pretty low boiling point. Of the four of us, Phil was by far the smartest, intellectually the most curious, and the most academically ambitious. He was already a pretty gifted linguist. Obie and I played JV baseball together and would both play varsity ball the next couple of years. He was a very interesting person.

For the life of me, I have little idea what brought and kept the four of us together for those few years in high school. Perhaps our diverse types was the attraction and humor the glue. If part of each was taken to be one the result would have been the perfect 1950's high school guy. Of course, we had many other friends, male and female, and did hang in larger groups. But it was rare that we weren't together in most social settings.

The "Bow"

The Rainbow was located on Varick Street in the space of today's Matt's Brewery gift shop. In the '50s, it was owned and operated by Stan Tencza and his wife, both terrific people. They were typical Polish- American hard-working types who demanded good behavior from their customers. Contrary to my Dad's experience at "the Bow," in my day there were no fights.

The Tencza kids, son John and several daughters, went to Hughes. I knew all but the youngest daughter from my grade school days. Phyllis and Geraldine were both very attractive. They and John were extremely nice kids.

John was in the Class of '59, and many of his friends gravitated to his family's bar, Brian included. Others as Jim "Butch" Musa, Bob "Link" Marx, Bob Spatuzzi, John "the Drifter" Hamlin from South Utica, Rich "Mugsy" Williams, George "Skipper" Cahill, Ron Wakeel, Harry Julian, Don Klosek and others formed the core group of "the Bow" high school crowd.

The Owl and I were the youngest of the bunch. How we made our way there, I don't really recall, but I suspect that my friendship with Brian had a good deal to do with it. The Owl, a West Utica kid, lived around the corner. He may have been a Bow regular already, as part of the Night Clubbers group formed by many of the previously mentioned guys.

The bar business was not limited to students. There was a healthy mix of adults who were regulars. The two groups coexisted in an interesting fashion. We took a hint from the older crowd and realized that drinking excessively was not cool, not to be tolerated, and would get you tossed. Stan Tencza did not tolerate misbehavior from customers, period. I don't remember any of us high schoolers ever getting drunk there. In fact, some eventually started to order soda. In our crowd, no rookie drinkers were allowed. All of the guys except for Gilberti and I were upperclassmen, and some were of the legal 18-year-old drinking age.

Far too many high school kids in those days got into serious, sometimes fatal accidents as a result of drinking and driving. But there was no such danger in hanging out at the Rainbow. My parents knew their underage son frequented the bar, but they did not mind, knowing the Tenczas ran a tight ship.

The place had a bowling machine of a shuffleboard type, and a section of tables for dining in addition to the long, beautiful wooden bar. It was a popular lunch place, especially for the brewery workers. The kielbasa and kapusta sandwich was the best in town.

It was strictly a male bar, and no one of any age took wives or girl-friends there. We pretty much used it as a first-stop meeting place before going on to a dance or house party. I would normally hitchhike on Genesee to Brian's house and we'd either walk or get picked up by an older guy to head to the Rainbow. One regular routine was to have a couple of beers before a St. Francis dance. At the dance, we'd hold our breaths every time Father O'Neil walked by. I don't think we fooled him.

Two Rainbow-related incidents had a lasting effect on me. They took place in either '58 or '59, but the dates are not important to the stories.

One night, four or five of us were standing at the bar and someone suggested going to Roach and Quins to hassle "queers." I had never been there and never gave homosexuality much of a thought. In the '50s there was no such term as "gay." The terms used, like "queer" and "homo," were derogatory.

Stupidly, I went along. At the bar, a couple of our guys got into an argument with two gay guys, who were very adult. One thing led to another and one of them challenged us to step outside. Of course, we did not hesitate since we were five and they were two, and "queer." We went across the street to a deserted parking lot. There, one of them pulled out a big gun. He aimed it right at one of us and started to talk. He gave a quick lecture about never being where you do not belong and never to make fun of something you know nothing about. The two of them left us standing there shaking and with our mouths wide open. I never again went to that bar for any reason. I also never again considered bothering, or making fun of, anyone who was not straight.

The second incident was, in a way, similar.

One summer day, I went to the Rainbow alone to check out who else was around. The only other guy there was Rich Williams, "Mugsy."

He was a very smart, funny guy who carried a good deal of weight around and came from a pretty wealthy family. At the time he was driving a little MG convertible. Rich suggested that we take a ride down to the black section along Oriskany Street. We did and parked right in front of the most popular black bar in the city, Wang and Gene's. The sidewalk was teeming with people walking back and forth, most of whom were carrying bottles of booze. What we didn't realize at first was that many were black migrant workers who came into the city from the local farms to have a good time, which meant getting drunk, many very drunk.

So here we were, two very white guys wearing Bermuda shorts and preppy shirts, leaning against an expensive sports car watching drunken black migrant workers go by. Not a good idea. A drunk approached us waving a big iron railroad spike under our noses. We froze, and I do mean froze, as he waved that spike closer and closer to our faces. A crowd had gathered and were all egging the drunk on. All of a sudden an arm reached in, grabbed the drunk by his collar, and violently threw him down on the sidewalk. The drunk recovered and took off, and the crowd dispersed.

The arm belonged to Cecil Brandon, one of my UFA basketball teammates, who just happened to be in the bar and saw what was happening. I hugged him, thanked him, and we got the hell out of there.

That was yet another lesson in not going where you are not wanted, where you might be thought of as looking down on or mocking others.

In the 1950's, especially before 1958, matters involving sexuality and race were not openly discussed or communicated in cultural venues such as the movies, TV, and music. The most popular films, music, and television shows were wholesome, dealing with love and family life, with some crime and Westerns thrown in. The top movies were ones like "Witness for the Prosecution" and "Vertigo," and the top songs were ones like "April Love," "At the Hop," and the Everlys' "All I Have to Do Is Dream." Also ruling the entertainment world were television shows like "Father Knows Best" and "Perry Mason." The fact that Raymond Burr, who played Perry Mason, and actors like Rock Hudson were homosexuals was kept secret, hidden, and disguised by the Hollywood and New York studios. "The Defiant Ones" with Sidney Poitier and Paul Newman was, in 1958, the first modern movie to address the racial tension in America. Popular literature also ducked social issues to a large extent.

At UFA, the topic of homosexuality never came up in student conversations, although some kids tossed insulting phrases like "you queer" to insult others. Students who may have been homosexual stayed in the closet. No one thought of teachers in those terms.

Racial matters are another story that will be discussed in more detail later in the book. In the halls of UFA, there was no racial tension or fights or animosity.

One day, a store owner who ran a soda and snack shop across the street refused to serve Ed Hill. Virtually the entire football and basketball teams went back there with him and waited until he got served. The owner served him.

Report Card Panic

Coincidentally with paying more attention to sports and having a good time, I ran into two subjects that gave my grades a huge jolt. I didn't hit it off with either Geometry or the class's teacher. Adding to my study misery was a Biology teacher who was old and hard to hear. I was not about to self-teach biology. She did offer those who chose to sleep during class a table at the back of the room. I found a spot at the sleeping table and learned next to nothing of biology.

So here I was, a high honors student as a freshman getting low grades in two subjects as a sophomore. Brian was in more trouble than I. He was flunking at least one course, Physics. And since he was a junior, his grades were important for his not-too-distant college applications. What to do? Neither of us looked forward to taking a weak report card home to be signed. We were rescued, sort of.

A female student who worked as a volunteer in the counselor office had access to blank report cards and just happened to be a master forger as well. She helped a few of us with a fake report card scam, forging names at both ends of the process. We took fake ones home to be signed, and then she signed the real ones to hand back in. Being very smart, we had her convert D's to C's, and C's to B's, in the courses where we were falling short.

But we were stupid in another way. Once you used one fake, you had to fake the rest of the year. Brian wound up committing the ultimate sin by flunking Physics, since he would have to retake it in summer school or risk not graduating the next year. He got caught at the end, had to 'fess up, and practically got jailed by his parents. But he didn't rat out anyone else. Thank God I passed Geometry and Biology, by the skin of my teeth. And in the eyes of my parents, I was still an excellent student.

I paid a price later.

The '58 Dating Game

In our day, what you did on a date was determined by whether you had access to a car or not. In 1958, I was one who did not. If I dated without doubling with someone who drove, my date and I had two choices—walk or take the city bus.

We guys had another option when going out, hitchhiking. Hitchhiking was common and by and large safe. Getting a ride by sticking out your thumb on Genesee was a sure thing. Only rarely did a potential problem occur.

Once in a while, a guy who had a questionable agenda in mind would pick you up. It wouldn't take long to figure out that agenda after you got into the car. Once you did, you simply said thank you for the ride as you hopped out at the first stoplight. That was it.

A Saturday night date for a non-driver normally meant two options: the movies or a house party. House parties were very rare.

That spring, I had started to date a neighborhood friend, Sheila Denn. Sheila and her St. Francis friends Karen Maher, Sue Zuccaro, Georgia Orth, Judy Noonan, and others were fixtures after school at the Square View. Obie had been sweet on Karen all along, and I knew Sheila well. The UFA guys, including our group, gravitated to the St. Francis girls much more than we did to UFA girls. To this day, I don't fully understand why, except that they seemed more fun and down-to-earth.

The Friar Tech girls were two-fisted beer drinkers, smokers, very good dancers, and had great senses of humor. They also encouraged group gatherings, including on dates. What it boiled down to was a bunch of friends having a good time, a "clean" good time. The view from our UFA side was that the Catholic school girls were wedded to the confessional. We had fun at dances while dating most Saturday nights.

Sheila asked me to her Junior Prom, an invitation I accepted. I was a first-term sophomore.

We were at a disadvantage since I did not drive. On prom night, we doubled with someone who did. All went well until it dawned on us that we could not go "up North" for the traditional carousing day after the prom. We had no way to get there since the couple we doubled with were not going. I was completely embarrassed and thought that might be my last date with Sheila. She seemed to be growing more upset by the minute as she contemplated missing out on a day in Old Forge with her friends. I think it was her mother who came up with the last-minute solution: take the train.

In those days, the Utica to Thendara run was an ongoing weekend service of the New York Central Railroad. Mr. Denn worked on the 4-to-11 shift as a dispatcher for the Utica train, walking daily to and from work. The family did not own a car, due to their large family size which presented the problems of both passenger capacity and money. We did take a lovely train ride, hitching a ride home with others, and had a good time. Why do I repeat the story? What goes around, comes around. After being shut down for a long time, the Utica to Thendara line not only came to life again but is now, nearly 60 years later, a very cool thing to do.

Getting back to dating in general: You never dated on a Friday night. That was boys' night out. If you met girls, you met in groups at dances or other activities like a house party. Saturday night was date night. For the non-driver, it was a downtown movie, which you walked to or reached by bus. The first-run, popular movies were downtown, where four theaters within walking distance of one another offered a variety of film choices. There was always at least one good movie playing. Our date routine was pretty standard and regular.

After the movies, we sometimes stopped at the South Utica White Tower for snack, or King Cole's for an ice cream if it was still open. In our case, the night usually ended on the Denns' porch talking. Nick would arrive after hoofing it up Genesee and ask, "How did the White Sox do today?" I never knew why he was such a White Sox fan, or if that was just his way of making conversation.

Once, we saw three movies at three different theaters on the same date. We did it with a late matinee, an early evening movie, and late show, running from the Stanley to the Olympic to the Avon. It was all done for less than ten dollars! In our day, most movies were good. The theaters were spacious and well laid-out, with beautiful fixtures and up- to-date equipment.

The Stanley has since been restored, so those who attend functions or entertainment there can see what it was like in its glory days, which did extend to the '50s. It was the gem of the region. The Olympic was a notch below that, but also a super place to watch a film. The two others weren't as nice.

The downtown was alive, even for teenagers on a pretty standard date in 1958. It was safe, fun, reasonable in price, and the place to go.

Do Ya Wanna Dance

Whether you were attending a school dance or a prom or dancing at a bar, there were just two choices, the slow dance and the jitterbug.

Only rarely did the slow dance look like the Fonz on "Happy Days." Whether you were dancing to Anka's "You are My Destiny," "Twilight Time" by the Platters, or the many other slow-dance love songs, there was usually space between you and your partner. "Embrace dancing" was rare. Yes, slow meant slow, but it also meant pace and a lack of dance steps. At many functions, if a boy and girl got too close on the dance floor, an adult chaperon or monitor would speak to them.

Most fun was the jitterbug. It could be as extreme as my classmate and teammate, Joe Prymas, when he jumped in the air, flipped to the ground and back up, and generally put on quite a one-man show. He flipped and flipped to "Great Balls of Fire."

But the favorite, and by far most attractive, style for the jitterbug was the one-two-three, back step, one-two-three back step move, with hips controlled in rhythm to the beat of the tune. The Proctor style was one-two, back step. Songs like "Peggy Sue," "That'll Be the Day," and "Young Blood" came alive to the jitterbug. The cha-cha did appear a tiny bit when songs like "Cherry Pink and Apple Blossom Time" played, but not many danced it.

Girls did not often dance with girls. At every dance, there were pretty large groups of boys who weren't dancing. Lord knows why they were there.

Dancing could be great fun. When you found a partner you could really mesh with, it made a night. It might be my imagination, or poor memory, but the St. Francis girls were better dancers than most from other schools. Perhaps that was part of their attraction.

The music was all about love—its tragedies, joys, rejection, and loss. "Teen Angel," "It's All In the Game," "It's Not for Me To Say," and "Who's Sorry Now" ran the gamut of teenage emotion.

At the semester's end, I swished a big "whew!" that I got away with my report-card doctoring and vowed "never again." With friendships of both genders solid and a decent year of sports, thoughts turned to summer vacation. As I mentioned in a previous section, the question was not whether you were going to work as a teenager but where. It was the same question with my summer sport, baseball.

Job, Money, No Work

One day, my father informed me that he was taking me to meet Dennis O'Dowd, the West Utica political leader. He was "Uncle Denny" to my father for well over a decade. Of course, he was not really an uncle but a political mentor and political boss who my father served.

Uncle Denny was the head of the Utica Board of Water Supply, the water board, which was the public water supplier for both the city and growing nearby suburbs. It was a regional service controlled by the city. Elefante controlled the city, Dennis O'Dowd was his man, and therefore Elefante, through O'Dowd, controlled the water. Watch the movie "Chinatown" and it will provide a very good feel for the importance and power of controlling the water supply.

A description of my summer job interview with Uncle Denny is provided in my book "From the Inside." I won't repeat it here, except to say that I landed a good job at the Board's construction yard on Kemble Street that turned out to be all pay, no work. It was as close to a no-show padded payroll job that one could find without technically being one. That summer, the steel-toed boots I bought for work were not necessary.

Work started daily with crews assembling in a big room inside or in the yard, with foremen taking their normal crews out and adding bodies depending on the day's project load. We, the few summer helpers, were never called. We got paid to do nothing.

The full-time workers were a cast of characters as interesting, entertaining, and outrageous as I have ever worked with. Shaky Jake, Big Dick, Johnny Inman, Clean Gene, Piss 'Em Up Howie, the Crouses (Buster and Ronnie), the Shraeder brothers, Butch Polera and many more were zany, funny, some corrupt, highly skilled, nice, and crude all at once. And that is just a partial description.

The most interesting days for me were the rainy days. The place came alive. Everyone stayed in the yard and at least one big poker game broke out. I fancied myself a good poker player. I was so good that I lost the equivalent of my first paycheck the first game I sat in— Welcome to the big leagues. I sure learned real poker the hard way. By summer's end, I could hold my own.

The Water Board was my first taste of a political patronage job and how the Utica political system worked. The full-time workers had to give a portion of each paycheck to "support the party." The paymaster from downtown headquarters showed up on payday to both pay and collect. We summer kids were exempt, at least directly. I had no idea what, if anything, was expected of my dad.

Summer Ball

Utica was a hotbed of baseball on all levels, including semi-pro in the Utica MUNY League, which played four nights a week to crowded stands at Murnane Field.

The league featured an assortment of ex-high school and college star players, current college guys, older sandlot-type players, and a few high schoolers. The league was top-notch in talent, spirit, and fan interest. Remember: in that era, baseball was clearly the national sport.

The perennial team to beat, Marcy State, has been described in an earlier section. Joining Marcy in the league were Mohawk Containers, Dick Smith's, Jan Roback Post, and Roundhouse Garage, as well as a team from Griffiss Air Force Base and at least one from the Ilion-Herkimer area. There may have been a couple of others, and sponsors occasionally changed.

Largely because my father knew the player/coach of Roback Post, Dick Model (Modliszewski), I had the opportunity to join that team. At 15, I was the youngest player in the league. Once again, I was on a team where it was unlikely I would see much action. My father viewed it as a learning experience.

Although he was on the older side of baseball age, Dick was still an excellent hitter, as was another aged star, Red Holstein. Ralph Polera, the Ruskowski brothers, Joe Tosti, and Fi Decosty, two recent Rome Free Academy stars, Jules Homekay, Ronnie Duda, and others formed the core of a very competitive team. That year I pitched only a few games and won them all. That included beating a very good Griffiss Air Base team in a rare Saturday afternoon game on the base. That was the only time that year I pitched against a tough team. Dick not only took it easy on the kid but righty gave many more starts to the veteran pitchers on the team.

Griffiss had outstanding baseball and basketball teams in the Utica municipal leagues. The Air Force brought in airmen from all over the country, which meant a revolving talent pool with a lot of turnover every few years. On the base, the good athletes also received special treatment from their commanders. After all, it was peacetime.

So, I did not play much. But what a great experience it was just to hang with the team. I recall going up to Old Forge to play the town team, followed by a party and a swim at Model's White Lake camp. His young son Bobby played the bat boy position. Bob would later turn out to be one terrific athlete himself. By the way, I pitched and we won the Old Forge game.

League games were priceless. Junie Romano and his constant chatter of "the hub, the old huba, huba", Alan Gilberti and Dick Miller lighting up the field with their talent. There was the gritty Danny Falatico, George Fanelli, the smooth John Giaquinto, and a whole bunch of East Utica guys who could really hit. Babe Lange from Ilion had a fierce curveball. He struck me out on three pitches the first time I faced him. Bill Larkin, a priest pitching under a fake name, was a terrific hurler and fierce competitor. He could anger you into confession by knocking you down if you got too close to the plate. Even Bobie Salerno came back to play before he became a Major League umpire. I struck him out once and he threw the bat right at me! The best local pitcher I ever saw, Don Churchill from Little Falls, pitched in the league for (of course) Marcy State. That year, rumor had it that he was offered a bonus deal to sign a big league contract but turned it down to finish school. The offer was said to have been $10,000, a large amount in those days.

Utica was a robust baseball city and I was proud to be a small part of it. Just being there, and feeling it, was a special privilege to a young teenager.

That summer was a period in my life far different from previous years. I was growing up. Near the end of 1958, Utica would also start on a path that would lead to its becoming a far different city.

Mister Fischer Comes to Town

Albany had finally had it! The Apalachin meeting bust and the relentless investigative reporting by Utica's Gannett newspaper finally called a halt to tolerance of an "open city" controlled by a longtime Democratic boss. Both the Democratic governor and the split legislature moved to take action.

The action taken was the naming of a Special Counsel to conduct a full criminal investigation of corruption. That decision was preceded by legislative moves in both houses, the Assembly and Senate's crime-related committees. Governor Averill Harriman then acted to carry out the will of the legislature buttressed by his own view that Utica politics and crime were out of control.

Why a special counsel? It was a near-certainty that the normal criminal investigative procedure, going through the county district attorney, would produce the same result as earlier investigations: zip. It was believed that the local DA was part of the very machine to be investigated, the Elefante machine. In the '50s and a bit before, it was common knowledge that the Elefante-controlled city was aligned with the Republican-dominated Oneida County government controlled by the leader of the county Board of Supervisors, the county legislature, Harold Kirch of Camden. In other words, there was a long-running belief that a, "you take the city, I'll take the county" deal was in place. It was critical to that deal for the Elefante group to control the DA's office, thus avoiding serious legal scrutiny of the ongoing corruption. The perceived rigging of the law enforcement game to thwart investigations and prosecutions, which frustrated the Utica newspaper and reform-minded citizens, came to an end when Albany stepped in. It is important to note that the described arrangement was believed "on the streets" and claimed by the newspaper but was never proven or documented in a serious way.

Harriman, a Democrat, turning on the city's Democratic regime? Yes, because Apalachin had altered the stakes. No politician could be viewed as tolerating the Mafia. Thomas Dewey had set that precedent as governor in the '40s; Harriman followed it. The handwriting was on the wall for the Elefante machine.

The special counsel appointed was Robert E. Fischer, a lawyer from the Binghamton area. The actual appointment was made by the New York State Attorney General at the time, Louis Lefkowitz, in accordance with state constitutional procedures. Harriman made the call and Lefkowitz picked the man.

Fischer's charge from the state was to investigate organized crime, gambling, governmental corruption, and vice in Utica. Interestingly to me as I look back on it, pinball machine gambling was cited. A high school kid playing pinball at Master's had no idea of either that activity's citywide and area wide scope or its seriousness. We did not give it two thoughts in our scheme of things, which was teenage fun, excitement, and taking a shot at winning some date and soda money. We teens were not lonely in our, don't care mindset.

Most of the people in Utica were oblivious to the ongoing corruption. Why? The city's crime rate was extremely low. Visiting a house of ill repute or placing a wager on a horse were viewed as victimless crimes in the sense that one had a personal choice in those matters. The Mafia murders of the '40s, like the Morelli case, had already disappeared from the city's collective memory. With a low crime rate and economic prosperity, there was no overwhelming public outrage or cry for change.

To repeat: If it weren't for the trooper stumbling into the Apalachin meeting and the fact that three men from Utica were in attendance, there likely would have been no special counsel and no investigation. Part of Utica's history from '57 on would have been quite different.

Anyone familiar with the television show "Law and Order," and with the histories of special counsels, will not be surprised at how the Fischer probe was run and how it played out.

After a relatively short investigative period, Fischer convened running grand juries and began to squeeze people starting with minor figures. Of course, he hoped to flip them, move up the chain and corral Mafia guys and Rufus Elefante.

Early casualties included Utica's police chief and deputy chief, both of whom resigned as they were being investigated and questioned by the Fischer team. People who operated houses of ill repute were indicted. In connection with that area of vice, Fischer went after "Uncle Denny" O'Dowd in 1959 in an attempt to oust him as water board head. He initially failed and my summer job was saved.

The Fischer investigation lasted four years, until 1962. All in all, there were 23 criminal indictments and 21 convictions. Uncle Denny was one of the last to fall. They had him on tape conversing with prostitution house operators and nailed him for obstruction or perjury. A couple of police officers, the madams and their bag men, some city officials in addition to O'Dowd, and at least one city contractor did short jail stints.

Not a glove was laid on any Mafia figure or Rufie. Fischer did not land a big prize. In terms of his long investigation, these targets were innocent of any wrongdoing. But make no mistake, the investigation had a major impact on the city and the area. To grasp that impact, the role of the press and Utica's local and national image must be understood.

The Utica newspaper's anti-corruption crusade picked up steam and heft. Gannett wisely smelled the large story of the Mafia connection to

Utica politics and sent in one of their young reporters, Jack Germond, to aid the local effort. Germond would eventually grow to be a national columnist and a fixture on the PBS show "The McLaughlin Report." The local, in-house reporting team consisted of Tony Vella and Bill Lohden. Both were excellent investigative reporters, and Germond made the team all the stronger. They did an amazing job of honest reporting, even while subject to threats of physical harm. The change that soon hit the politics and psyche of the city would not have happened without the reporting of the Utica newspapers and their three key reporters.

Their stories and the early stages of the Fischer investigation drew national news coverage to Utica. It was not pleasant or sympathetic, to say the least. Utica received the labels of "Sin City" of the East and "the city that God forgot." I think both labels were coined at the "New York Journal." They stuck. The image of Utica as a prosperous, religious, fun city on the move was supplanted by the dark image of a city of crime, vice, and corruption, a city of sin. That image was spread nationally.

The Utica Observer Dispatch, headed by general manager Henry Leader, won a Pulitzer Prize in 1959 for "a successful campaign against corruption, gambling and vice in the best tradition of a free press." Investigative reporting was carried out in the finest tradition of journalism.

Although the legal story would not be completed until 1962, the civic and political stories were set by 1959.

Some National Matters

Our president was at the end of his second term, his finale, as the world and the country were becoming more complicated. Domestically, a fierce budget battle broke out between those who favored a balanced-budget approach to control growing inflation and those who championed the growth of federal spending. By the 2017 standard of a $20 trillion national debt, that argument seems quaint. Ike is turning over in his grave.

There were two international issues that were getting more serious by the day. One was the possibility of a war with Russia over Berlin; the other, Castro gaining the upper hand in Cuba in '58 followed by his march into Havana in 1959. Both were extremely troubling to the country as a whole, and to Eisenhower (who was also physically impaired).

Mirroring the organized crime issue in Utica was the effort by various elements in the national government to go after the Mafia figures identified at Apalachin. These efforts did not involve the Utica attendees, but were centered more on the New York City-based crime families.

With a presidential election looming in 1960, a young senator from Massachusetts continued to make his national name, an effort that first arose in the '56 Democratic Convention. Much later, it would be fascinating to see revelations about the various relationships involving JFK, Cuba, and the Mafia.

CHAPTER 5

'58 –'59

A Typical Day at UFA

What a special place UFA was. Most of us couldn't wait to arrive on the steps of the Kemble Street building every morning. A description of a day in the life of a UFA student may serve to recapture the essence of school life in our large building, occupied by about 2,300 students and scores of teachers plus a few administrators. These are but a few memories of school life.

The day started at 7 a.m. with an effort to catch the early Sunset Avenue bus, filled with UFA and St. Francis students. Most of the guys on the bus eyed the girls and talked about their looks. If you missed that bus, you headed to Genesee for a later bus and, while waiting, stuck your thumb out for a ride. More often than not, a commuter headed to work downtown gave you a ride. Pity for us in the cold winter meant more rides. We added to our discomfort by not wearing hats. A hat was not cool, but our ears sure were.

Arrival at school was at least half an hour before the 8:30 bell rang. In the winter, you stood in groups with your friends in the well of the entranceway and partway up the stairs. A spot next to the radiator was a prize, most often captured by Jim Musa and Bobby Marx. God knows how early they arrived to grab it. In warm weather months, we gathered along the side of the black iron fence in front of the school. Virtually all of the guys gathered in our group were jocks. These early morning clusters were not coed and not racially integrated.

Nearly every day, Owl held court. The rest of us laughed as he worked his routine, insulting everyone who walked by or was late in joining us. A nod, being tweaked by, the Owl was prized by those outside of the group. We enjoyed his daily routine.

When the bell rang, you headed to your assigned locker room while greeting friends, of course paying most attention to the girls. UFA was blessed with some very good-looking girls. Most of them you knew by then, although some you did not. A smile and a "hi" from Cindy Hart, Mary Semararo, Jackie Pierce, Rose Ann Dziura, Sue Pecham, or Pam Levine was the perfect way to start classes. The cutest was Pat Dmochowski, who was also a cheerleader. For obvious reasons, we called her "Patti Alphabet." She and Jerry Lysik eventually married. Another cheerleader, the cute, perky Theresa Carlone had a daily happy greeting. Some of good lookers had no idea who I was. But, they sure got a daily stare from me.

Stashed in your locker were coats, extra books, and the other items you couldn't lug around all day. The locker room atmosphere could also be fun. You might share the room with Hughes school friends like Phil Newman, Ellen Lasher, Harvey Cramer, or one of the Adasek brothers. If your locker happened to be next to a freshman's, you razzed that freshman. In '59, my locker neighbor was a very cute freshman. I practiced slamming her locker shut before she had a chance to use it. She looked exasperated daily. I wonder if she realized I was flirting with her.

The halls were jammed with teachers, students, and administrators, all hurrying to their positions. Our principal, Art Wildes, was a behind-a- closed-door kind of guy who you only saw at school assemblies and events, or when he was meting out punishment.

His rules enforcer was the ever-present assistant principal, Austin T. Bell. He is best remembered as a big guy carrying so many keys hanging from his belt that they seemed to dominate him. He must have carried every key to every room in the building, along with his car and house keys! Little did he know, but they made so much noise that it tipped his bathroom raids, to catch student smokers, so far ahead of his pounce that they always had time to douse the cigarette in the john and flush.

The first classroom stop was homeroom. Mine was Room 245. The homeroom teacher took attendance and sent you on your way to classes. The same homeroom and teacher stayed with you for the four years. I was blessed to have Betty Pritchard, one of the nicest ladies I have ever known, as my homeroom teacher. Joe Prymas, a close friend and baseball teammate whose last name, like mine, began with a "P," sat next to me.

Most of the teachers were interesting and understanding, but firm. A few were too old to still be hanging around. Ethel Peas, an English teacher, had taught my father. I never had one of her classes, but a couple of my friends did, and swore that she could not hear a word they said.

Second-year Latin took me to Ruth O'Brien, who was not in the same league as "Mag," sweet but not as tough. My Latin slackened, but the class was a charge. Vic Falcone dazzled with his translations, and one girl perfected a fainting spell every time she was not prepared for a spot test. Those of us who may also have been less than ready rooted for a spell that would wind up taking most of the class time. The girl operated like a repetitive fine-tuned clock, but Miss O'Brien always took it seriously. We students, to borrow a future Reagan quote, thought "there she goes again" as she collapsed to the floor. Yay, no test!

Citizenship class was taught by Miss Perritano. As mentioned earlier in the book, she miscalled the reign of Castro, to say the least, but she ran a great class of open discussion and debate about current events. She and Sylvia Hinds of the same department were two of the best in the school.

I didn't yet have either as teachers, but two relatively young ones, Miss Dybas and Ms. Picolla, were attractive in their own ways. Flirting with them became an enjoyable game to play. My guess is that they viewed those of us who did as silly.

One annual gym activity no guy ever wanted to miss was the square dance classes led by Coach Swiecki. He loved leading the class, since he got to select his partner. You can guess that he always picked the prettiest young lady. We also angled to grab a doll for a partner— sometimes, but not often, failing. The classes were full of laughs and the only time gym was coed. Swiecki seemed to have even a better time than we had. I can still see his big, broad smile as he promenaded around the gym floor.

Study hall and gym class were very kind to athletes. If you wanted to get your homework done, a study hall presented a good opportunity. That year I often seized it. If you simply wanted to hang around and shoot the breeze somewhere, you got a pass from a coach excusing you from study hall and joined guys sitting around the coaches' office. The coaches also didn't mind if a varsity athlete skipped gym class and sat around the office.

Guys, including me, occasionally got caught and penalized by the principal for skipping study hall in favor of the gym office. I could never understand why. It wasn't like we were skipping school or even leaving the building. Plus, the coaches who allowed this practice were staff.

The silly part of it all was that many non-athletic students perfected the art of study hall-skipping in various ways and went to hang around the Square View, smoking and drinking cokes. We, jocks, preferred hanging together with our coaches and together. As I got older, I often wondered if the school administrators ever realized how myopic they were, cracking down on kids who went to the coaches' office but not those who went off campus.

The tone inside the classroom was respectful, orderly, and friendly. Some wonderful friendships developed and others were resumed. Kids I hadn't gone to grade school with, like Lynn Rettig, Marie Degni, Diane Kalin, Bill Cosgrove, Linda Kennedy, Patti Glinski, and Jim Hyde were smart, interesting kids who brightened nearly every class. And the chance to see and interact daily with so many of the old Hughes gang was a particular joy. Bob Garver wore a permanent big smile. Stew Pratt, Barbara "Brooksie" Brooks, Stew Roberts, Judy Burke, and Bart Gorman became lasting friends. At a much older age, Stew Pratt and I played a good deal of golf together and I often acknowledged him as my "oldest" friend.

There was such closeness that even much later in life, you could often pick up a friendship where it left off. For example, if I did not see Dave Berkeley in years, the minute we did come into contact our friendship would still be strong and lasting. Decades later, Stew Pratt reminded me that I should have listened to him and not played in that football game without wearing equipment. Bart Gorman gave me great legal advice later on, and "Brooksie" and I chat of the old and new as we bump into each other around town. John Cahill eventually moved back to Utica and can be found hanging out at Panera Bread or Barns and Nobles; he's still as nice as nice can be. Jim Musa later banked our money under the Gold Dome when it was the Savings Bank of Utica and while taking my money on the golf course on Saturday mornings. Thus, strong bonds formed at UFA have been everlasting among many of us. I even joke with Gloria Dybas, still a fine- looking woman, about my mediocre performance in her Spanish class. To this day, she shakes her head the same way she did as I stumbled through a translation.

The End of the School Day

Whenever possible, we headed for the Square View as the final school bell rang. My friends and I could be found there just about daily, except during baseball season, when there wasn't enough time to hit the Square View and also walk to Murnane for baseball practice. During basketball season, practice started at 4 p.m., which allowed about 45 minutes to squeeze in socializing. We usually used that time to talk with the St. Francis girls or dream up schemes to terrorize Howard, the owner. We once loaded Brian's hanging jacket with salt and pepper shakers. When he stood up to leave, some fell out and the others were visible right in front of Howard. He blew his top, thinking that Brian was stealing salt and pepper. As a bunch of us nearly fell over laughing, even he realized it was a joke and smiled. I always thought that beneath all his bark, Howard was having as good a time as we were. He and his son, who ran the place, were really very nice to tolerate us. They sure did not make a lot of money off of us!

The Magic Season

Being a part of the '58-'59 edition of the UFA varsity basketball team led to an unforgettable experience in sports and race. The school's yearbook describes that season as "history making." When Coach Collins, the season before, stated that next year he would "be loaded," he believed his vision of building a championship team would come to fruition. Collins had a "feel" for team-building not to be found on a blackboard or in a diagram. That, combined with his ability to inspire his teams to win for him, made him a great coach.

Before describing the team and the season, a couple of aspects of high school basketball should be discussed.

We played in two formal leagues which were the most elite in the region, the City League composed of the high schools within Utica, and the Central Oneida League. There were only two divisions, A-B and C-D. The A-B teams were part of the city and county leagues. The City League included the teams from Utica Free Academy, Proctor High, St. Francis, and Utica Catholic Academy. The Central Oneida League consisted of those city teams plus New Hartford, Whitesboro, and Rome. In the post-season, the two Catholic schools played in a parochial tournament while the rest played in the Section 3 tournament. There was no statewide tournament for any leagues or levels as there is today.

Neither shooting governed by time clocks nor a three-point line existed on any level of basketball, anywhere in the country. As a result, scores were lower on average than they are now.

In the years when I played, including that season, UFA was the only school in the Utica area with black players. Virtually all black students of high school age attended our high school.

It could be argued that the level of play at that time was the highest in local history. In addition to the then greater talent pool of a more populated city and area, coaching and talent came together in a special way. There was also an advantage in the fact that most good athletes played only the big three sports: football, basketball, and baseball. Athletic ambition, among the better athletes, was not spread around to what were then considered minor sports. High school hero status, and most college scholarship opportunities, resulted from excelling at one of the three major sports.

The talent in those sports was deep, the competition was fierce, and the stands were packed. Those stands were packed not only with students and parents, but also with sports enthusiasts from the community who followed and supported the teams. The results were intense rivalries and excited fans.

LUCKY U, LUCKY US

After intense tryout and practice periods, the UFA varsity season that year started out pretty normal and ho-hum. The starting team had Chris Harrison, Larry Taylor, Ed Hill, Morris Allen, and Milt Boddie. I was the first man off the bench. Chris and Larry were half-term students, meaning they would graduate after Christmas break and become ineligible to play. Coach Collins pulled me aside after most of our early games to tell me to have patience while waiting for my coming time to start.

In the first phase of the season we went 6-2, losing close games to New Hartford and UCA, both excellent teams. New Hartford was led by Warren Palmer and his younger brother Kenny, Steve Lockwood, Lou Zangrelli, and Pete Morris. Warren was the best individual player in the area. He went on to be terrific player at Hamilton College. Ken also later played at Hamilton. Steve was an excellent three sport guy who also went to Hamilton quarterbacked their football team.

I had the pleasure of becoming a good friend of Warren as we grew older, playing with him for years on the Utica MUNY basketball team along with players like Mike Damsky and Ed Hill. Very sadly, Warren passed away unexpectedly at too young an age. Fittingly, the last I saw him was when we played a pickup game shortly before he died. He was a great guy and a good friend. Steve Lockwood is a local attorney, a community activist and a friend.

That season, UCA had a super starting lineup. Pete LaClair, Jerry Stys, Tom Kent, Dick Veath, and Mike Dyer formed a team that had little weakness. The last three were former Lourdes stars.

Although Chris and Larry left our team, we grew in strength. There were two reasons. Neither was tall or a great shooter. They were good players, but did not offer the kind of mix to the team that would result in a championship season.

After their graduation, our starting unit was Hill, Allen, Boddie, Brandon, and me. We blended perfectly in several ways. All of us were relatively tall, Morris was the best defensive player around, Boddie was a wonderfully athletic guy who could rebound with anyone, Hill was the best all-around guard in the leagues, and Brandon and I could score from way out. Cecil Brandon was also an excellent rebounder and a skilled high jumper on the track team. I had a decent all-around game while being a highly skilled shooter. Hill, Brandon, and I provided the scoring punch while Boddie and Allen added their specialties, defense and rebounding. I was the only white starter.

Boddie used to show off in gym classes by taking on a group in volley ball single handed and beating them. Brandon broke school high jump records saying to girls when asked how he jumped so high, "It's all in the terminology, baby." Hill excelled at three sports including being one of the school's best half backs in history.

I don't know how it happened, but we immediately meshed as a smooth, fluid, unselfish team. My guess is that there were three reasons: Hill, Coach Collins, and race. Hill was the best athlete on the floor and could easily have averaged well over 20 points a game. Instead, he sacrificed his individual scoring, distributing the ball to make sure that anyone could score at any time. Simply put, he was a great, unselfish passer. Never once was the race factor mentioned by anyone on the team. We had mutual respect, peppered with a good deal of fun kidding about who was the best of the best.

We were a loose bunch. Collins encouraged both our competitive instincts and our looseness, with gimmicks like having shooting contests to win free game tickets we could give to family and friends. Our bench was critical to our team unity. They didn't play much, but cared and practiced as if they did. Our sixth man, Jerry Lysic, was a highly respected student leader, and a football star and varsity baseball player to boot. He never complained about playing time, and he gave 100 percent, as all of us did, when he got into a game. He even taught me the "spit shine."

Cecil and I most often led the scoring. Morris was a funny case. He would not wear his glasses, which he needed, on the court and could not see well enough to shoot well from the outside. But he did see well enough to stay on the chest of the opposing team's best offensive player and shut him down. Allen was tall, could move, and practically lived inside the jocks of the player he guarded. In all the years I played ball, I saw and played with only one other local player who guarded like that—Nonnie Pensero.

Defense was our key. Coach Collins didn't teach it to us; we developed it on our own. We played a switching man-to-man, kind of a zone/man- to-man hybrid, with Allen never leaving his guy. Since we were all of good size, we weren't often overmatched when we switched. That year we gave up, on average, a very low 43 points a game!

I still recall the first game we played with our dream team in place. Why? It was against St. Francis, and my girlfriend and several of the other Friar Tech girls my friends and I hung around with were cheerleaders. We won that game 71-41, with us starters not playing much of the last quarter. I couldn't miss from the outside, and scored 20 points. We were all in a rare zone, playing near-perfect ball. The one time I looked at the St. Francis cheerleaders, I saw stunned faces with jaws dropped in disbelief. The Friars were a good team, too, with players like Ed Macner, John Prendergast, and Mike Brown.

The new starting lineup went 12-0 for the rest of the regular season, having only one close game, the second game with UCA. It was played at the small Kernan school gym, our opponents' home court— UCA was such a small school that they could not justify, or afford, their own gym. The gym was so packed for the game that the cheerleaders were sitting right on the playing floor.

That game had a bizarre moment. We were down by a few points with about five minutes to play. At stake was our win streak and, most critically, the city championship.

Collins called a time-out. It was our practice to sprawl on the floor before game huddles and during time-outs. But when we fell to the floor this time, Collins went nuts. He started yelling and screaming, even pulling our hair while cajoling us to win. The black guys then went equally crazy and started to yell and chant. We escalated to the point of not even realizing what we were doing—then got up, went out, and won the game by four points! That final drive was as much a spiritual experience as it was a basketball game.

Tiny UCA, a school of a couple hundred students, gave us, a team from a school of more than 2,000, the most trouble. Their guard, Pete LaClair, was the only guard at the time on any team who gave Hill trouble; and Stys, Veath, and Dyer were all tall, tough, good players. Their coach, Shorty Powers, instilled a motivation similar to what Collins gave to us. We were slightly better shooters, though, and had Allen's unique defensive talent.

With the City and Central Oneida League titles in our pockets, we went on to the sectional tournament. After defeating Proctor and New Hartford, we were set to play Holland Patent on the neutral court of New Hartford. That game merits special mention for a couple of reasons.

Our team had captured the fancy and interest of the Utica community. We had won 14 games in a row and were getting plenty of newspaper ink. A team anchored by four blacks and one white inspired special curiosity, interest, and good will. Anywhere I went carrying my UFA duffle containing my sneaks, socks, and jockstrap, whether hitchhiking to school, standing at a bus corner, or stopping into a store, I was asked about the team, the last game, and the next one. People always wished me the best. It was like a miniature "Remember the Titans," the Denzel Washington true-story football movie, Utica-style. Coincidentally, our school nickname was also "The Titans."

As a result of the heavy fan interest, the UFA-Holland Patent game of 1959 became the first high school game broadcast on the radio in our area. Lloyd Walsh, a wonderful man who was the WIBX sports guy, called the game while seated in a standing-room-only crowd.

Although Holland Patent had a good team led by Gus Jones, Cooke Hoffman, and Ronnie Payne, they were outgunned. Cecil and I killed them from the corners, each of us scoring over 20. Hill ran 'em all over the court. We won, 73-54. Next stop, Oneonta and the regional semifinals.

The Oneonta Yellow Jackets entered the game with the same 18-2 record as ours. It was played at the Colgate University gym, with a heavy snowstorm pounding outside. Both the pre-game and start of the game were dispiriting to us.

When we ran onto the court for our pre-game warmups, we were met with dead silence. None of our student body fan base was there, nor were many adult fans. We were wearing our years-old away-game uniforms, which were pretty ragged, to put it mildly. We felt as flat as flat could be.

Oneonta came out to the roar of their crowd as we were taking our layups. They looked splendid, in beautiful satin sweat suits. Their first two players were dribbling basketballs painted with their school colors, which they dunked. We stood watching. This time, our jaws dropped. They were something to see. And we hardly knew where Oneonta even was.

Their stars, the 6-foot, 6-inch Bob Turell and the 6'3" or 6'4" Jim Konstanty Jr., were the two biggest guys we would had faced to date. Although we had balanced size as a team, Boddie and I were the tallest, at 6'2." Brandon and Boddie could dunk, but only with a volleyball. Their hands were too small to palm a basketball.

At the start of the game, it seemed that only a few seconds had expired and we were down 8-0. All of a sudden, the gym doors opened and busloads of UFA students and fans marched in, all shouting and cheering. The buses had been delayed by the storm. The court action paused.

We came alive, cut the deficit, and the game was nip-and-tuck the rest of the way. We put it away in the last two minutes, when I snuck under the basket unguarded, was hit with a perfect pass by Hill, and scored easily in the split second the play took. And we did not relinquish our three-point lead in the final seconds.

Turell and Konstanty went on to play for Cornell. I also got to see and know another member of the Oneonta team, Larry Santos, when we met as students at Colgate. Larry became a successful singer/songwriter, of all things, and even wrote some of the Four Seasons songs. He also did some well-known TV ad ditties for major companies like Chevy and recorded some good songs as singles. One went as high as #36 on the charts.

As an adult, Jim Konstanty Jr., the son of the excellent major league pitcher Jim Sr., practiced law in Oneonta. We bumped into each other on occasion at events in Cooperstown and both recalled "the game." In the small world of upstate New York, my wife and I befriended Jim's sister Helen and her husband Dave Reese, who shocked us one day when they informed us of his passing. We had no idea.

At 19-2, we reached the finals of the class A-B sectional tournament, to be played at the Syracuse War Memorial arena against West Genesee, a Syracuse-area school. They were 20-1 and featured two players who were possibly and were good enough to have been high school All-Americans that year, Loren James and Frank Legg. Both would play at Syracuse University after high school.

As we warmed up for the game, I got the basketball shock of my young life. A group of guys from the Syracuse Nationals, the NBA team, climbed into the stands to watch the game. There were Dolph Schayes, Red Kerr, Larry Costello, Hal Greer, and Al "Blinky" Bianci— all watching us play!

We lost the game, which was much closer than the final 71-58 score indicated. Legg and James did not beat us. The fact that they had ten decent players they ran in and out of the game did. We actually led by a couple of points at halftime, and the game seesawed until the second half of the fourth quarter. Then, within a matter of seconds, both Allen and I fouled out. We had lost our legs, as it's called. When that happens in basketball, you start to reach with arms rather than move with legs in your defensive play, which means you foul. Their superior numbers ran the five of us into the ground. After Morris and I fouled out, Hill played his heart out trying to carry the team. At one point he stole a pass, dribbled the full length of the court, missed the layup and virtually collapsed. I never forgot that scene. In my research for this book, I read the Utica newspaper account, which noted the play and called it the point where we lost the game. "West Genny" had too many guns for our five to handle.

Readers may wonder why so many words should be devoted to that year's team. The reason extends beyond basketball, although I thought it important to pay homage to one of the decade's great local teams. Early in the next season, that starting team went 7-0 before Hill and Allen were lost to mid-year graduation. Our record spanning all of 1959 was 27-1. That was among if not the best record of area teams to that date. It was accomplished in an era of no separated classes of school types. You played every good team. Many would argue that our "five" played as a team better than any five in the area's high school basketball history.

The rest of the team, Jerry Lysik, Lou Sandouk, Bob Garver, Larry

Habble, and Ray Laduc were, like me, white guys who could not jump. All contributed to our team fabric. Although there was no racial tension on the team, race does cut to the heart of its story.

Racial unfairness and other forms of discrimination existed in the school system and the off-court behavior of the team. Both were part of the times and of Northern segregation, which was milder than the awful Southern brand, but nonetheless discriminatory.

Hill, Boddie, Allen, and Brandon all graduated from high school. But none went to college. I did. All could have played some level of college ball. Why didn't they? None took high school courses that made them academically eligible for college acceptance. Like most blacks at UFA, they were placed in "shop courses," where students were taught trade skills, not prepped for college. They had no opportunity to demonstrate their academic potential or interests.

Most white students in the '50s didn't attend or graduate from college either. Less than 20 percent of whites earned four-year college degrees. It was possible to get a good job with a great company, like GE or Bendix, with a high school diploma. A high school education meant a good deal in the '50s. Schools and their personnel were ill-equipped, or not all that motivated, to assist or inspire students. Black students were doubly cursed, by being stereotyped right out of the gate as not college material.

UFA coaches did not get involved giving academic advice, or in marketing players to colleges. There were no letters of support or tapes sent, whether one was a black or a white player.

In four years at UFA, I recall meeting with a guidance counselor just twice and taking an aptitude test indicating that I was a perfect candidate for a career as a forest ranger. It got to be a joke when it became known how many future forest rangers could be found at UFA.

In addition, parents who hadn't attended college had little skill in assisting and directing their children. Although my parents never even finished high school, there was their assumption and encouragement, going all the way back to our Jay Street years: My sister and I would be educated. The black perspective, in an age when people of color were still being lynched in the South and discrimination remained obvious in the North, allowed little faith that the system would be either fair or encouraging. It's clear that a black American's definition and vision of aspiration was usually very different and more complicated.

I got to know Ed Hill well, and continued to know him well for most of our lives after UFA. We played local ball together, socialized together, shared some politics together, and even volunteered together. Ed did turn noticeably bitter in certain ways as he aged. It was clear to me that he was convinced he did not get a fair shake in high school, and that this cost him a shot at college. He could have been an outstanding Division II or III player, and some schools did recruit him. The minute they learned he lacked sufficient academic credentials, they walked away. There was yet another problem, which many young athletes in relatively small areas faced. I suspect this one remains today.

When an athlete is a big fish in a small pond, he tends to have an inflated view of his talent. In the case of a good high school athlete, that often results in false assumptions and poor decision-making. Several of us on our basketball team, who also excelled at other sports, assumed we were good enough to be chased by colleges and that our sports abilities could overcome academic deficiencies. Certainly Hill, Brandon, and I felt this way. Cecil, for example, actually thought he would play for Syracuse University. There was no one who could or did tell him otherwise. I never learned whether Ed Hill was guided with sound advice and disregarded it or not. I know I had no such help or frank direction. In high school arenas, egos are easily inflated. That inflation is often encouraged, not tempered, by adults.

LUCKY U, LUCKY US

At the end of my high school career, in the fall of 1961, I was invited to visit and try out for a basketball scholarship at Saint Bonaventure College. At the time, they were ranked #2 in the country behind the Ohio State team of Lucas, Havlicek and Bobby Knight. Even working out with the freshman team I realized I had no business being there. I was not even close to being a Division I player. Prior to that visit, no one put me in my proper place in understanding the realism, meaning limitations, of my talent. Adult direction was just not there. There was a more important social component that impacted our lives.

Family life was a strong pillar of society in the 1950s, for all races. All of our team's black players except Brandon had solid families. It is no coincidence that Hill, Boddie, and Allen did well in life. They had good jobs and contributed to their families and communities. Ed Hill worked for years with troubled kids, served on the Utica City Council, did volunteer work, and was a very well-liked and respected guy. Milt Boddie had a long career with Niagara Mohawk, now Nationalgrid, and had a son. Morris Allen went into the service, lived in Texas, and I think did well. I occasionally bumped into one of his brothers, who spoke highly of Morris's success. Cecil Brandon came to Utica from the outside. He had no family here that we knew of, and was rumored to be much older than his birth certificate indicated. There is a funny story to tell that might have suggested those rumors may have been true.

A custom before every game was that the varsity team sat together in the stands to watch the early part of the JV game. At one game in the UFA gym, we were all assembled but Cecil. At one point he came in, strode over to us, and asked if we would like to meet his wife. We weren't sure whether or not he was throwing the famous "Cecil baloney." We said: Sure, bring her over. He did, introduced the woman as his wife from Detroit, and we all politely greeted her. She looked well into her thirties!

Brandon was sharp and quick of mind. He also had a certain charm to him. But even in high school he lived on the edge, cutting corners, and wasn't even shy about it. He was a very sharp dresser and wore more jewelry than was common in those days. He did not appear to have a part-time job, as most of us did. He has lived a life in and out of jail. What a waste.

My wife, Ed Hill, and I helped him at one point of personal tragedy that he experienced, but received neither a "thank you" nor a notice of where he was off to. I hope he is alive and settled into a peaceful life.

Cecil was unusual, in those days, in having no family. Today, with 72 percent of black children raised in fatherless homes, no one should be shocked that these kids tend to have a steep mountain to climb in life. Segregation was a sin and a stain in the '50s, but I'm not sure the breakdown of the family is not all that much of an equally destructive problem.

Segregation was practiced in Utica too and on the UFA basketball team of '58-'59. It was shameful and embarrassing to look back and realize that we gave it little thought or notice at the time. The minute we left the locker room, we separated. No black player came to Garramone's for pizza, none were invited to the "Bow," no black joined us at the movies, and I didn't invite one of my black teammates to my house. We were completely segregated socially, and we thought nothing of it. I did not know, nor have I ever asked, how my black friends and teammates felt or thought about this. That was Utica in the 1950s. The banality was the sin.

A Mistake Comes Home to Roost

My sister, then a student at Cortland State College, was dating a Hamilton College basketball player. He and a couple of teammates followed my high school team that season while attending as many of our games as they could. I also took in some of theirs.

The Hamilton guys were frequently fed Sunday dinners at our house. They lobbied both their coach and me on behalf of their team, the Continentals.

The Hamilton coach was Ken Patrick, who also worked as a high school basketball official including refereeing some of our games. He knew me and I knew him.

When I became a junior the following fall, Coach Patrick wanted to arrange an early admittance deal for me at Hamilton. I turned it down. Why? Two reasons. The primary one was the fudged report cards of my sophomore year. I was scared to death that my deceit would be uncovered and that my whole world would know I lied.

My inflated athletic ego also entered into the picture. I believed that my skills and appeal would take me beyond little old Hamilton College. I was thinking of a bigger, more well-known college level of play. I did not realize at the time that I was strictly a Division III talent.

We were left to our own devices in those days. Mistakes in judgment, so frequent with the young, were made in the absence of the mature common sense that might have guided both our conduct and our decision-making. We grew up fast; in that respect, too fast.

1959 Baseball Season

Our baseball team completed the trifecta of UFA, winning all three city titles in 1959: football, basketball, and baseball. The baseball title was deceiving, because we did not have the best team—Proctor did. We were very good, but they were excellent. With players like Joe Marci behind the plate, Dickie Detore at first base, Mike Mancuso, Rich Brindisi, Sammy Zito, and Pomp Delmonte, Phil Scampone, Larry Sardelli and Rock Asselta, they had a top-to-bottom lineup that was hard to match—except that we did when it counted.

We beat them 1-0 in a game where I pitched against Pomp. He lost a one-hitter while I gave up a few. Years later, he told me that Pete Pace, the Proctor coach, put a ball in his hand and told him to "go get us" the following week. That story implies that we were to play again. I have no recollection of a second game and could not find it reported. It is, however, possible that we actually tied for the city title. I hope we did, given Pomp's one-hit loss. We pitchers know how heartbreaking that type of loss is.

One of our better players was my basketball teammate Ed Hill, who played third base. He demonstrated what a great athlete he was the day he ran in a track meet at Murnane, then sprinted over to the other side of the complex, put on his uniform, and played third base—he competed in two separate varsity sports in one afternoon. Another talented baseball player, Jim White, was also a very good running back on the football team. Our pitching rotation of Jim Ward, Art Swartwout, and me, with Obie and Pete Palewski as relievers, was excellent. Joe Prymas, Steve Mitchell, Tom "Tick" Price , Doug Virkler and Bruce Bullock all played the game at a high level. We were a notch below Proctor in talent, but good enough that we could beat them on any given day. The aspect of the rivalry I best recall is how much I liked the Proctor guys and considered them friends. Many still are.

In the summer, Whitey and I were selected to play on a local team that would be taking on the visiting Yankees Rookie Team of that year. The Yanks put together a team of their top minor league prospects, which barnstormed around the country playing local all-star teams. Our best high schoolers from the Utica area joined other good players, many from the MUNY League. I'll list the high school guys as an indication of how high the level of play in Utica was: Tom Kent and Fran DeJoseph of UCA, Fred Brindisi of Proctor, Billy Roemer and Jim Young of New Hartford, Gus Jones from Holland Patent, Manny Laura (the great Ilion High catcher), Frankfort's Tony Conigliaro—one of the area's better all-around athletes, Whitesboro's Hal White Jr., Ed Macner and Fay Billings from St. Francis, we from UFA. We lost the exhibition game, but it was a thrill.

From One Ball to Another

Whenever I notice a high school student today attending a Senior Ball, I think back to the St. Francis ball of '59. The differences are striking.

Both boys and girls asked for dates, depending on the circumstances—which ball was being held at which school. Obviously, UFA boys could not ask to go to St. Francis events. But even same-school invites could come from either a guy or a gal.

The balls, in general, were held at a school gym that was decorated by a student committee. The St. Francis event that year, I think, was held at Twin Ponds country club, which was also decorated by a student group. I do not think St. Francis had a gym. Student committees selected the bands. There were not yet any local rock bands, so an older-style dance band, always Lawrence Luizzi's, played. It was comical to hear them try to play the rock tunes of the time. They were as odd-sounding as the singers on "The Hit Parade" as they covered the top songs of the day. Think Snookie Lanson singing Blueberry Hill.

The boy had the job of arranging transportation, renting his tuxedo, and buying a corsage for his date. The couple either drove in a car, doubled with someone who drove, took the bus, or got a ride from a parent, usually a father since many mothers did not drive. There were no limos to rent. I don't recall knowing yet what a limo was. Although I never did it, my friend Brian and his date did ride a bus to a UFA ball once.

All males dressed the same. A tuxedo and all the trimmings, down to the shoes, were rented at Vitullo's. The jacket and the dressy,

French- cuffed shirt were white. The pants, clip-on bow tie, belt, shoes, and socks were black.

The variation among the girls was more pronounced, but only in color and in minor ways, such as whether the shoulders were covered or not. The Dick Clark Company had described the female look as "bouffant hair, bouffant skirt, fussy, frilly and oh so feminine." Not too far off, except the St. Francis and UFA gals were short on the bouffant hair while more of the Proctor girls resembled Connie Francis and Anette. A good way to picture the gowns is to watch "Gone With the Wind" while imagining them sticking out about two-thirds less and as somewhat shorter. Very little skin was shown, due to the floor-length skirts and modest tops. It was the "debutante" look. All were dressed modestly and in good taste. Some of the best prom gowns were sewn by mothers.

The '59 ball started for us with pictures taken at the homes of a couple of Sheila's friends. I recall the session at Barbara Maranti's since I knew of her dad, a politician, and was thrilled to meet him.

I have no recollection of the dance or where we went later, but it was common to hit White's Inn in Chadwicks, near New Hartford, where the music was good and proof of age wasn't checked. Quite honestly, the balls themselves were dreaded by most guys, who just looked forward to the post-ball drinking and, if you were lucky, necking.

I do remember, from that night in '59, our last stop at about 2 a.m. at the Parkway Eagle, the famous landmark on the hill. There were five or six couples in our group.

The Eagle was the prime necking spot for teenagers who drove. You kissed at the Eagle, since your date's father was up when you brought her home, making a goodnight kiss difficult. But that night not a kiss was had, because all of us, at least a little tipsy, started rolling down the hill fully dressed. We did it several times. Little did we realize that our jackets, the rentals, would be grass-stained. My mother took mine back since we were longtime customers, and Tony Vitullo said not a word.

Since I'd gotten my driver's license a few weeks before, at 16, I was able to drive up north the next day. The days of the Thendara train were over. We did have to return home by 9 o'clock, since that was the legal witching hour that defined forbidden nighttime driving for those who were under 18.

Utica Free Academy—A Special Place

UFA, with over 2,300 students, was a melting pot of all types, talents, and interests. We were a miniature version of Utica, with a sense of community, UFA community, uniting us. Although parts of our community were closed, like the fraternity of jocks, we all came together in the hallways and the classrooms. In the years I spent as a student there, I recall no violence, no fights, no drugs, and no weapons, not even serious arguments. We all got along, most enjoying friendships and daily good cheer. As an athlete, I was privileged to know both white and black students of both genders well. Racial relations among us students, across the board within the halls of school, were positive and without tension. The overwhelming majority of students practiced respect for each other regardless of race, gender, or any other differences. Lasting memories and friendships were the special gifts that UFA gave me and many, many others.

That high school also gave us a view of a melting pot city that was not available in many ways in those days given the ethnic identities of neighborhoods. In UFA we of different races, religions, ethnic backgrounds and talents lived from early morning to dismissal under one roof. The unique value of the school at that time was preparation for the more integrated, diverse time and city on the horizon.

Playing team sports at UFA presented another lifetime gift, the bonding of athletes from many schools and communities. School rivalries, race, ethnicity, religion, none of that interfered with unique friendships and respect among the city's athletic community of players, coaches, parents and fans. These relationships have lasted a lifetime as have the stories and recollections. The exaggerations have grown with age.

Uncle Denny Comes Through Again

The end of the school year quickly merged into the start of summer employment. I returned to the Water Company. Since 1959 was a mayoral election year, Rufie and Uncle Denny loaded up on summer employees as a way of generating votes, even with the Fischer investigation underway. A bunch of college and high school kids were hired for the Kemble Street yard. We even got Brian a job.

Some genius in the company's hierarchy had the idea of forming one crew out of the summer group, and to have it led by a couple of the college guys. We were assigned to cut grass at the Graffenburg Reservoir, about a mile and a half up the hill from the Parkway. We were given our own truck and equipment and sent on our way daily.

The reservoir, now Camp Sitrin, was set pretty far back from the road with a long, tree lined driveway and a thick block of tree between the road and water. It was out of site, the perfect spot to dog it.

Of course, the first thing we did was to cut a lot of grass—to create a whiffle ball field. With a bat and a ball sneaked in, we started to play after about the first hour of grass-cutting.

At noon sharp, we jumped into the truck and went to lunch at a little place at the corner of Graffenburg and Higby roads. It was owned and operated by the sister of a Water Company foreman—the toughest one, Tony Labuzette. For about two weeks, tops, we followed the same routine, which included drinking beer at lunch. We would drive back down the hill a bit smashed and immediately sleep it off on the field. I vividly remember coming down the hill one day and nearly missing a big curve. That day I was the one driving, and I credit the good Lord with preventing an awful accident.

We turned out to be far dumber than the genius who had the idea of a crew of students in the first place, by not realizing that Tony's sister would rat us out to her brother. She did.

One morning, a cavalcade of black cars and a couple of trucks drove up the driveway and raided us before right after the first whiffle ball pitch. We were busted. Our initial punishment was worse than getting fired. I, for example, was immediately driven to another company field, given a hand-held hole digger, and shown where to dig. I was left there the rest of the day, and told in very harsh terms to have those holes dug.

I had no work gloves. You didn't need them to play whiffle ball. To dig holes in the ground, you sure did. I dug, twisting and turning and then shoveling up the loose dirt. By the end of the work day, I hadn't completed the job. Tony himself picked me up and smiled when he saw my bloody, blistered hands. I knew immediately that they were never going to put fence posts in the holes. It was just severe punishment. I learned by whispers back at the yard that all of us young jokers were given similar jobs for that day, some worse than mine.

As we left work, Brian and I were told by Big Dick that we would become part of his pipe-laying crew starting the next morning. I was actually happy that I was going to be a real construction worker. The image of shirt off, cigarette in mouth, working a jackhammer was, in my mind, about as manly as it got.

When I got home, my mother almost fainted when she saw my hands. I told her only that it was a tough day at work and that I was a jerk to leave the yard forgetting my work gloves.

We spent the rest of the summer doing all kinds of jobs: running a jack-hammer, loading and delivering a truckload of pipes to job sites, being flagmen, digging out trenches, and other demanding, hard but fun, tasks. Today, my wife and I reside on Graffenburg Road not far from the old reservoir. Every time I drive by it, I think of the Water Company in 1959.

Big Dick was a serious but great guy. Shaky Jake, Piss 'Em Up Howie, "The Syrian," Freddy Brewer, Ronnie Crouse, Clean Gene, and a few others were very funny, knock around guys who told hilarious stories and treated Brian and me as if we belonged with them. I loved them and the job. I still think of them and their stories, most of them not clean enough or appropriate to the book.

I would have a summer job there for one more summer before the Fischer investigation finally got Denny ousted. I was also blessed to work at the headquarters downtown during Christmas vacations. There, I filed old water bills and payments. I vividly remember the Water Company's 1959 Christmas party, with a smile and a good laugh.

It was an annual affair, held in the upstairs office of General Manager O'Dowd. The food and drinks flowed. "Owl" was spending the night at my house for a reason I do not recall, so I invited him to meet me at work at the end of the day to do some Christmas shopping down-town. I hadn't planned to attend the party, since I was not a full-timer. But the ladies I worked with, Mrs. Burke in particular, pushed me to join the fun, even suggesting that I bring my buddy along. We went.

At one point, I looked over and spied Owl with a drink in one hand, sharing cigars with Uncle Denny. They stood side by side as Christmas music played, having a good old time. Here was a sixteen-year-old high school kid pressing flesh, sharing a drink and a smoke, with not only the head of the Water Board but a big-time politician under investigation!

We left the party, both feeling a bit good. I had the bright idea to take a walk down to the Boston Store to tell Santa what we wanted for

Christmas. My mother ran the store's beauty shop, which was pretty close to where Santa sat on his Christmas throne.

The downtown streets were packed with shoppers, all smiling and of good cheer as we wished everyone we passed a Merry Christmas. Charities were collecting coins on the street corners, people were loaded with gifts in their arms, and the smell of the Nut Shop was strong as we walked by.

We hit the beauty shop as our first stop, said hi to my mother, and flirted with some of the girl employees. All of them, including my mother, laughed, my mother not showing even a bit of irritation at our obvious drinking.

We did see Santa. Owl sat on his knee as they both cracked up laughing. The Genesee bus ride home was filled with shoppers of good cheer. Most even joined in as we led the singing of "Jingle Bells." Christmas season in downtown Utica was as good as it gets.

The Summer of '59

To return to proper calendar order: The summer of '59 began with the Water Company job, nightly activities with friends, and a more regular spot in the Robak Post team's pitching rotation. When not playing, I occasionally watched a MUNY League game with my father. After one game he stood up, told me he wanted to walk home, threw me the car keys, and said: "Don't be too late." It was his signal that I could drive at night once in a while. But my mother would set serious limits. Her limit was "No." Some of my friends had turned or would soon turn 18. Others took Driver's Ed at UFA and were licensed to drive at night at 17. Cars and rides were somewhat restricted by age, but more often by one-car families. I do not recall one time when I or any friend was stopped by the police while driving underage. By that summer, rides were no longer an issue for us most of the time.

Having access to a car opened an opportunity to frequent two of Utica's top spots, the iconic Kewpie's on Oneida Square and White's Inn located in New Hartford, where most of us went to drink and dance. Our group rarely went to Kewpie's, however. Many kids thought you had to be very drunk, and go late, in order to tolerate the place's dirt and its rough regular clientele. White's, on the other hand, was a date destination when a car was available. But our favorite gathering place that summer was "The Fence."

The Fence

The daily routine for me was to work all day, play a baseball game at night if one was scheduled, and finish the evening at The Fence. It was a two-tiered white wooden fence on the right-hand side of the King Cole ice cream parlor exit on Genesee Street? Every night, Mondays through Thursdays, 10 to 15 of us gathered to sit on or stand around the fence to talk, laugh, kid around, and listen to music heard from car radios driving by. If you watched "Happy Days," just picture an outdoor Arnold's.

We started with an ice cream cone or milk shake (a "black and white" shake was my favorite), took it to the fence and spent the next two or three hours socializing.

The group was girls and boys from St. Francis, UCA, and UFA. Most of the female crowd were from the Catholic schools, and their core consisted of Sheila Denn's friends. Sheila, Karen, Sue, Georgia, and Judy were all regulars. I recently bumped into Maureen Denn, Sheila's older sister, at Mass and described the fence. Her high school group, she said, didn't use it. She did, however, speculate that the fence was an offshoot of "the wall" at St. Francis where students congregated before and after school. That got me thinking that UFA's versions were the winter radiator spot and the outdoor iron fence. The "fence" on Genesee was the summer extension of a regular school gathering place.

My male group expanded to regularly include the funny, entertaining Bill "Poncho" Walsh from UCA. Owl now had some entertainment competition. Others such as Bill Mahady, Chuck Sears and others moved in and out of the gathering. Most of the time, though, Joe and guys like Tommy Geronimo who had their own cars, drove around the circle, over and over. The ice cream parlor was an island surrounded by the drive around.

With car radios blaring, those of us at the fence heard all the top songs of the day, like "Venus," "Mack the Knife,"

"Lonely Boy," "Mr. Blue," "Donna," and so many others. To me, the best song of that summer was "Kansas City."

At the Rainbow that summer, Owl performed "Kansas City," singing along with the jukebox while beating on his "guitar," a broom. The ovation was deafening.

A nightly question at the fence was whether or not East Utica thugs would appear. At times, they came looking for a fight. One of the ploys they used was to get out of the car, then have one of their biggest guys put on sunglasses and use a cane while the rest helped him around as if he was blind. One word from anyone making fun of the "blind guy" meant a trip to the train tracks in a dark area on the side of the property, then to be punched out. It didn't take us regulars long to figure out that game. We fence-sitters always took a deep breath when they drove away, staring at us as they left.

As the girls sat and the guys stood, a good time was had by all every night. We were never once asked to leave by King Cole's owners or managers, and the police were never seen. We behaved. It was all about friends, laughs, and fun.

Some of us, both guys and girls, created a little game we played every night until we tired of it. We thought we were very funny. The

Uptown movie theater was a stone's throw from the fence. Someone figured out that the last movie showing was playing right at the time the crowd at the King Cole gathering was breaking up. We then timed the rounds of the movie usher, who we named "Flashlight Freddy," and realized we could sneak into the theater to watch the last ten minutes for free. We spent night after night watching the same ten minutes of the same movie until we knew every word. We thought we were a clever bunch. Flashlight Freddy was probably laughing at the stupid kids who watched the same ten minutes every night. We were as goofy as the parents who tried to sneak kids, or the kids who tried to sneak friends into the Kallet Drive in Movie Theater on the truck route in New Harford. They always got caught.

The summer of '59 was the most perfect I ever had to that point in my life. I embraced being part of the Water Board crew of zany yet hard-working guys. My pitching in the MUNY League was now more regular as part of a rotation, pretty good for a young guy. In Sheila, I had a steady girl who shared most of my interests and did not mind walking on dates. I got the laughs, at both the Bow and the fence. Most of all, I had a group of friends—Brian, Phil, and the Owl who were special and inseparable. But I was also to experience one of the saddest, most empty moments of my teenage life.

The last day of that summer, which to me was the day before school started, I walked to the fence thinking a group would be there to share the end of a special time. Only Bill Mahady was there. King Cole was deserted.

I heard "It's All in the Game" by Tommy Edwards. It is a song of love that does reappear but the song does have a message and sound of sadness to it. My summer to that point seemed endless and with no sorrows, problems or disappointments. When young, the thought that fun is everlasting fools in the short term.

My stomach ached, my heart sank, with the realization that my "love" was actually that summer of '59 itself, and that it was forever gone. I realized that my life would change in profound ways. Brian and Phil were both entering college. The week before, I had taken Sheila to the train as she left for school in Albany. I knew that it would not be long before the college girl dumped the high school boyfriend. I was right. And I knew that the fence would never again be filled with such joy, fun, and good will.

Not too long ago, I had a talk with a friend's daughter as she was about to return to college. I remarked that she looked a bit sad. She said she was, because she had so enjoyed her summer at home. Her job, her family, her dog all seemed so wonderful. It flew by, and a certain sadness, of realizing it was now over, set in. We agreed that a perfect summer is a great gift.

Such was the summer of '59.

The Fall and the Fall

The autumn of '59 was a lively season in national affairs. Rocky, the new governor was setting up to challenge Nixon for the presidential nomination in 1960. JFK was going to battle for his party's nod. Dinah Shore was back on TV. Hedy Lamarr was that year's celebrity, showing how to get rid of that stubborn belly fat. Mario Lanza died at 38; Ginger Rogers hit Broadway. Russia and Cuba were getting hot, and Dear Abby was running lives with advice. The Dodgers beat the White Sox in six games, Ike weakened physically, and the blue-chip stock market was at $220. The economic boom was slowing down. The USA added Hawaii and Alaska as states.

In Utica, the mayoral election would mark the beginning of the fall of Rufus Elefante, who the Observer Dispatch labeled the city's "political dictator" during the campaign.

There is little doubt that the Apalachin meeting, which prompted federal and state investigations all over the map, including the Utica focused Fischer probe, was the cause of the political earthquake that would hit in November.

Over the years, Elefante not only exerted total control of the Utica Democratic Party, but also controlled much of the city's Republican Party through East and West Utica allies. He had actually started out as a Republican, in the late '20s. By the late '40s, there was no longer a legitimate two-party system in the city. Until 1959, the local elections were a sham.

In '59, a reform movement of reform-oriented Republicans, encouraged and supported for years by the Utica newspaper, finally gained control of their party's nomination process and nominated their candidate, Frank Dulan, for mayor. Yes, Dulan the ice man from my boyhood's Jay Street days, now an auto salesman, would lead the reform ticket.

The incumbent, John McKenna, bowed out. He and Elefante wisely figured their connection was too strong to withstand the likely political damage from the corruption issue. And corruption was the key, actually the only real, issue of the campaign. Elefante had a new, "clean Gene" face by the name of Leo Wheeler nominated as the Democratic candidate. By October, the war was on.

The Utica newspapers were lively, to say the least. Bill Lohden and Tony Vella wrote hard-hitting columns in addition to their reporting. The goal of the newspaper and the Dulan campaign meshed as one--- rid the city of Rufie Elefante.

An OD editorial made the interesting comment that the usual ten-day mayoral election season was starting in early October this time! Today, some of them start a year before. But back then the observation was telling, because previous elections were so wired and predictable that they were sham, requiring no more than a ten-day campaign.

If you were a mayoral candidate opposing a political machine run by an Italian boss, relatively soon after Apalachin and while a special investigation was going on, what issue would you run on?

Dulan took the corruption issue by the throat—Elefante's throat. He pledged to bring a new government "without probes," a government of the people, not by the boss. He put forth a program to restore both city financial accountability and honest bidding for city contracts. All of his issues pointed at the "boss." Interestingly, though, he rarely used Elefante's name. He didn't have to; everyone knew who he was talking about.

The OD beat the drum for a high turnout, calling it a race between "political henchmen" and "good citizens, the good people against those who, in the paper's words, "brought shame" to the city.

"The Ice Man Cometh" Dulan, had arrived. He won by nearly 4,000 votes, and would be sworn in as Utica's mayor just as a new decade began.

That election was the beginning of the end of the political reign of Rufus Elefante. He did control the city's Democratic Party until his candidate lost a mayoral primary to Dominick Assaro in 1967. But here, as in most cities throughout the nation and state, old-style machine politics was on the way out as the new decade began.

The Utica of the 1950s was also coming to an end, an end that would not be a positive one for the city. But ... from the stoops of Jay Street, to Hughes school on the hill, to the sandlot of Parkside, to Wankel Field. From the halls of UFA to the zany Water Board. From a beer and a pickled egg at the Bow to a dance. From the glory of baseball and basketball games to flirting at the Square View. From dancing to Pat Boone and Johnny Mathis, to shooting pool to Buddy Holly. With all the good and the bad, the easy and the tough, the safety of neighborhoods and the evils of organized

crime, the wins and losses, the romances and the breakups, the jitterbug at proms and ice cream at the fence ... growing up in Utica
in the 1950's was quite a trip, one I would gladly take again, and
would not trade for any other.

Epilogue

The Nation

It is not this book's purpose to judge decades or generations. Its description of the 1950s offers a remembrance of what was, a picture for those who did not live it, an opportunity for readers to make their own judgments of the past and of what has occurred in America since.

The conservative, rigid '50s were followed by the 1960s, one of the most radical decades in American history. Virtually every facet of American life started to change

The societal pillars of family, hard work, religion, manners, civility, and even formal dress started to erode. The rot that ultimately replaced the '50s culture is undeniable. At the same time, racial and gender barriers, so glaring then, have been torn down. In many other ways, though, today's standards aren't acceptable or even recognizable to those of us who grew up in the '50s. We are of the past, much more than we are of the present. Indeed, many younger people view our decade as backward, badly flawed, and in some ways evil. We do not. Nostalgia tends to brighten and soften memories.

However the decade is viewed, it is gone. No nation or society returns to the past. History always marches on. That, however, does not mean that past traditions and values cannot be resurrected. The good may be rediscovered and recovered while not repeating the bad. I do hope that what should be agreed upon as a universal good, the value of the complete family of two parents producing and raising kids, can be recaptured as the major American value common to all classes and types of people. No society can prosper economically or culturally without a strong, healthy family unit. I hope today's and tomorrow's America will relearn that lesson so engrained in our society of the 1950's.

It would also be nice to see adults dress as adults again!

Utica

The Utica of the '50s is also lost. Politics had little to do with the city's decline. Rufus Elefante, to his credit, ran a well-taken-care-of city in many ways, with excellent basic services. Utica was a place that most residents enjoyed. The city featured fascinating characters if not character. Utica was a city of intoxicating charm fun, wit, flavor and prosperity. In contradiction, it was also a city of crime and corruption. Both the city and its beautiful Parkway boulevard were two way. Monumental changes were taking place that would ultimately lead to the end of the city as we who grew up as part of it knew.

The first, and by far most important, was the flight to nearby suburbs. It was historically Americans' urge to reach for more open space and what was perceived as more freedom. A suburban single-family house, on an acre or half-acre plot of land set back from neighbors, became part of the American Dream in the '50s.

The postwar Baby Boom contributed to the need for more family space. The GI Bill provided low-interest housing loans, while all levels of government initiated infrastructure projects—roads, sewer facilities, water facilities—that encouraged the population spread. Many of the projects I worked on my last two summers at the Water Company involved laying water pipe in areas like Whitesboro.

As more people left Utica, the burden of city taxes and city costs increased since the tax base was shrinking. At the same time, Governor Rockefeller was spending a lot of money, thus driving up state taxes. Migration out of the state followed. Many New York cities were negatively impacted.

The national government's political power was also shifting to the South and West as powerful congressional committee posts also like many New York residents "went south." Griffiss Air Force Base was soon to lose missions and jobs.

The air conditioning that made Southern regions more livable, high labor costs in the North, and upstate New York's cold winter weather all contributed to the exodus of business and jobs.

As business left, the city and area lost a good number of the managerial class from companies like GE, Bendix and others. This not only eroded wealth but deprived the city of a rich talent base that had contributed so much to civic life.

All of these forces were starting to work against Utica as the decade ended. They would continue over the years, and more problems would pile up, contributing to the decline of life in our city. The loss of unique Damon Runyon characters of the 40's and 50's that made Utica special has been part of the overall change and decline. The city is now boring compared to years passed. The Olive Garden cannot hold a candle to Nash's or Grimaldi's. The Brewery gift shop is nice but it is not the Rainbow that existed in the same space as described in this book. St. Stan's, along with many other city churches, are closed. Those still in the business of soul saving and searching feature a good deal of empty pews. Temple Beth El is no more, the building having been repurposed.

These are but a few changes that lead to the inescapable conclusion that Utica is a shadow of what it once was. Its future is to be determined by the new and the young. If that future even approaches the city that was, it will be a bright one. Let us have hope.

The Worst and the Best

If anything could describe our view of life to come as the curtain was coming down on the decade of the 50's, the word optimism would apply. After all, we were growing up in one hell of an optimistic decade. We were to learn much too soon of the harsh cruelty that is often part of life's journey.

The two o'clock in the morning call I received from the frantic Mrs. Bigelow, informing me that Brian was killed in an auto accident, remains the worst call I have had in my life. Brian, Bill "Poncho" Walsh, and Fran DeJoseph, Utica College students in the early '60s, were killed in a head-on crash. Ironically, they were hit by a drunk driver who had left the bar to which they were headed. It was the same bar in Frankfort, described earlier in the book, where my date and I went after my first high school prom. I have thought of Brian throughout my life. I still miss him.

Brian's death also taught me a hard lesson in fate. The very day of the accident, he had stopped in to visit me at the downtown Chicago Market, located on Franklin Square where I was working part-time. We were to do inventory all weekend and were short of help. The store manager, who knew Brian and I, asked him to pitch in and join us and earn some extra money. Brian balked, saying he had promised others he would go out that night! To this day, that story is difficult for me to tell.

Phil, Obie, handsome and so very smart, was godfather to my second son. He experienced serious health problems and did not reach the age of 40. Life did not treat him as peacefully as he deserved. And I often wondered if I could have reached out to him more.

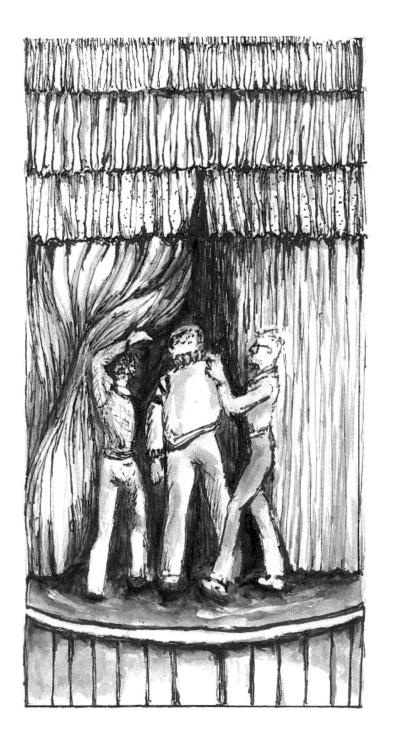

I was Owl's best man at his wedding, where Phil was an usher. Robert "Owl" Gilberti married Janet, his high school sweetheart, had a nice family, worked for New York State and led a life in local sports as an official and coach. He never lost his humor or his good heart. He had a severe stroke and passed away at age 55. What a great gift of laughter he gave all who knew him.

I say a prayer at Mass every week for Brian, Phil, and Owl. They were the best! I was blessed to have them as my close friends. Losing a close friend is forever a stark reminder of one's own mortality. But nothing changes the bond of friendship we were so fortunate to have shared in that very special decade. That bond has never been forgotten and is forever valued as a unique gift.

Utica Free Academy is also gone. Although it cannot be argued that school consolidation was unwarranted, the fact that the Utica School Board didn't retain part of the name of Utica's first public high school, so important to all who walked its halls, was a stain on the rich history of Utica.

It might be bumping into people on the street or in a coffee shop, emailing old friends living elsewhere, seeing UFA classmates at our 50th reunion or getting a phone call out of the clear blue. Whenever I talk to anyone who grew up in Utica, New York, in the 1950s, the same is said: "We were lucky to grow up in the time and place that we did." We sure were.